How to Be Unlucky

How to Be Unlucky

Reflections on the Pursuit of Virtue

JOSHUA GIBBS

CiRCE INSTITUTE

CULTIVATING WISDOM & VIRTUE

For Jon Paul.

It was the least I could do.

Contents

From Lethargy to Lectern 9

Death as a Practical Problem 35

Fortune, Luck, and Salvation 75

Temptation and Besetting Sins 107

On Pedagogy 143

On Pleasure 165

On Metaphysics and Freedom 195

Why Do Anything? 213

CHAPTER ONE

From Lethargy to Lectern

There are few issues about which American Christians are more confused and less consistent than the matter of goodness. I was embarrassingly old by the time I first heard a robust answer to the question, "Why be good?" A man wants his little son to grow up and become a good man. He wants his son to get a good job and marry a good woman. He wants to attend a good church and to believe the doctrines his church espouses. He wants friends, and even if his friends do not attend the same church he does, he wants to say of a certain friend, "He believes different things than I do about God, but he is still a good man. He loves God, takes care of his wife, and loves his children." On the occasion of his tenth wedding anniversary, a man enjoys taking his wife out for a good dinner, and when his little daughter begins to cry at having a babysitter and an early bedtime, a man says, "Be a good girl and run along." We do not like bad men, bad movies, or bad milk. Neither are we uncertain about what makes a man bad, for bad men cheat on their wives, lie to their bosses, steal from the tithe plate, and get drunk on Good Friday, while good men are honest about their faults, courageous in the face of death, courteous to women, and capable of profound generosity. So long as an American Christian is discussing the world casually with his friends, he talks sense on the subject of goodness.

However, if there is an open Bible nearby, one should not expect a man to speak lucidly of goodness, for an open Bible will remind the man that "all have sinned" and "none is righteous," and his discussion of goodness will turn to gibberish. He will tell you that all sin is the same, all sin is absolute, and that serial killers and saints are no different in the eyes of God. He will set aside all the passages of Scripture which declare that Noah was "blameless," or that Abraham was "justified by works," or that Lot was "just," or that Job was "perfect" and "upright," or that numerous kings of Israel "did that which was right in the sight of God," or that St. John the Baptist was "just and holy," or that Jesus Christ Himself spoke of "the righteous" on many occasions. Rather, he will claim with some pride that so far as God is concerned, our good works are nothing more than "filthy rags," and that every act of generosity or charity in human history has been tainted by secretly selfish motives. He will tell you "only God is good" and that God refuses to "share His glory with another," and then he will prove to you just how holy God is by describing the kind of eternal and excruciating torture a man deserves for committing the most trivial of sins. In fact, God's goodness is more or less incomprehensible apart from fantasies wherein elaborate pain is dreamed up for the most benign of sinners, as though the louder such suffering is declared "deserved," the more clearly God's goodness is seen. The wickedness of man is so complete and so total that God is either incapable or unwilling to enable man to do good. Any passage in Scripture which seems to suggest that what a man does with his life actually matters is written off by the atoning work of Christ, for we do not believe Christianity is a religion which helps a man fight temptation, but a religion which helps man get away with evil. We are apt to say these things when studying the Atonement or the Fall, and then turn around and expect our sons and daughters to wash the dishes, study hard, refrain from drugs, read their Bibles, abstain from pornography, and keep dignified opinions on art and music. We castigate "man pleasers," condemn selfishness, tell our children that God cannot be pleased, but then tell our children to not behave like animals. For whom?

Our problem stems not from an ignorance or disinterest in goodness, for so long as he is not pretending to be a theologian, the average Christian speaks of Goodness with genuine common sense. So far as the moral instruction of our children is concerned, then, every time we step into a church nave we take back everything we have said in our homes. Our children come to see virtue not as a necessity, but as the preference of adults, for the vices of teenagers tend to complicate the lives of their parents. Having proven to our children with theology and Scripture that good works do not ultimately matter, or that good works are impossible, we instruct them not to cheat, lie, steal, or curse. Telling our children that Christ has commanded us not to do these things does not so much dignify the law as it makes Christ's commands seem arbitrary. When I have made this complaint in the past, I have often heard it said there must be two kinds of morality, two kinds of Goodness, and that when we tell a child to "be good," such goodness has nothing to do with what Scripture means when it speaks of Goodness. However, if the Goodness spoken of in Scripture has nothing to do with telling a child to "be good," what passages in Scripture are actually about our lives? When Solomon writes of trees, rivers, the wicked, the king, the seasons, and the heart of a child, we take him at face value, and yet when he writes about "the righteous man," he is speaking in mere abstractions? This strikes me as profoundly arbitrary, although perhaps arbitrariness is simply an ingrained habit of modern religiosity.

The goal of education is to grow the student in virtue, and Christians of different ecclesiastical traditions already agree on what the virtues are: faith, hope, love, wisdom, justice, courage, and temperance. But why seek after the virtues? This is the divisive question. For the teacher, there is no more important question to address.

While "I made dinner tonight for my family" may not strike you as an impious statement, we are living in strange days, and from time to time I make some benign claim about a good thing I have done and find those around me taking up theological arms. In the last twenty years, significant changes have struck the grammar and vocabulary of American homiletics. If I am not mistaken, many Christians now want to hear "I made dinner for my family tonight *with the help of the Holy Spirit.*" We are not always insistent on that pious little postscript, although, once again, an open Bible nearby will spook us. We are sometimes willing to overlook a purely secular claim of having made dinner, but if a man finally beats an addiction to liquor, or stays faithful to his wife in the midst of a separation, or even if he makes a focused effort to not curse and enjoys a modicum of success, we insist God be openly, directly, and singly named as the source of that success. We are dismissive of the methods, programs, prayers, habits, and ascetic practices a man uses to overcome temptation because we believe any attention given to such things takes attention away from God, Who is entirely, directly, and simply responsible for the success. The Holy Spirit is not a co-laborer, but a direct cause. Similarly, if a former drunk describes the day in which he "came to his senses" and realized his life and liver were ending one bottle at a time, many Christians are offended that he has quit liquor "for himself, and not for God."

Most Christians draw a heavy line between doing something "for yourself" and doing something "for God," and with good cause. In the Sermon on the Mount, Christ teaches that those who do their good works before men "have received their reward" (Matt. 6:2), but those who do their good works in secret will be rewarded by their Father in Heaven. We have a choice, then, between being repaid for our good works by men or God. The choice is entirely our own to make. Rewards are pleasant, and so we may either enjoy a life full of rewards now, or else perform our good works in such a way as to defer payment until a later point. Christ confirms that it is better to wait in pain and hope. We should note that Christ simply assumes human beings are interested in doing good works, even while their motivations for doing good are diverse. However, the righteous man does not perform his good works with an ignorance or disinterest in their outcome. Neither does the righteous man lack a motivation to do good, for in the Sermon on the Mount, Christ lays out simple, forthright strategies for His disciples to follow that they might pray, fast, and give alms unto eternal rewards, and not be robbed of lasting rewards by cheap earthly imitations.

Christian conversations about good works have become sadly entangled with secular notions of altruism. Many Christians now assume that a good work is only genuinely good if the man who performs it has no thought of any good it might ultimately bring him, even if that good is union with God in Heaven. We are worried by the idea that there is any advantage in doing good works, because if there is, then we shall have to feel bad about not doing them.

Nihilism has become so ingrained in American Christian ethics that the idea we should do good works "for God" is interchangeable with the idea we should do good works "for no reason at all." Within such a framework, even the idea that putting your faith in God offers some benefit becomes questionable. If we should not think of the rewards God will give for acts of love, why should we think of there being any benefit to faith—confident, though we are, that we are saved by faith alone? The idea that we should do our good works "for God" is desperately in need of investigation, then. When I do the dishes "for my wife," I mean that my wife will benefit from my doing work that she would otherwise be doing. Because I am doing the dishes, my wife Paula can read a book, and given that reading a book is a leisurely activity and doing the dishes is mere labor, my willingness to do something low allows my wife to do something lofty. But what does it mean to do something "for God"? If Paula is benefitted by the things done "for Paula," is God similarly benefitted by the things done "for God"? And yet, Paula enjoys things done "for her" because she is a finite person, with limited resources of time and energy. When I do the dishes for her, I have saved her time, energy, and hassle. The omnipresent God cannot benefit from saved time, though, for God is beyond time. Neither can an omnipotent being enjoy saved energy, nor can an omnibenevolent being enjoy a reduction of hassle. Who then is benefitted by good works performed "for God"?

When we are not performing our good works "for God," we occasionally perform them "for God's glory," though it is difficult to say which of these expressions is the more under-explored. Too often, claims of doing this or that "for God's glory" liken God to a massive orb of light somewhere in outer space which glows just a little brighter whenever we pray or give to the poor. The selfless nature of a good work is thus proved by its ultimate irrelevance, given that no human being will ever see the divine orb of light glow brighter. Granted, such a suggestion sounds absurd, but does the average American Christian know any better what exactly happens to God when we glorify Him? Is there some deficiency in God's glory that human beings must add to it? This does not sound proper, but if man cannot add to the glory of an infinite God, what does it mean to act "for the glory of God"? What exactly is *glory*, and if we cannot add to the glory of God's being, where exactly does the glorification of God occur?

Human separation from God is further confirmed in our desolate, lonely understanding of what it means that Christ "died on our behalf." While nothing in human history could establish deeper bonds of unity between man and God, our fear of good works has led us to reimagine the death, burial, and resurrection of Jesus Christ as God's supreme act of alienation. Christ did what we cannot do, and the perfection of Christ reveals all our good works as filthy rags in the sight of God. Christ has not empowered us to do good works, or to enjoy divine love. Rather, Christ has done all the good works and the Cross is little more than a divine optical illusion whereby the Father looks at the Son but sees Man. There is no theosis, but an intentional bureaucratic error on

God's part, of which we are the witless beneficiaries. No real transformation occurs, no real rebirth, and no change, merely the appearance of all three. Christ dies "on our behalf," but He nonetheless commands His followers to take up their crosses and follow Him. When we treat the Lordship of Jesus Christ as a fact to be proved, a conclusion, and a telos, the Christian life is not a race to be zealously run in pursuit of a prize, but a run-down-the-clock situation wherein we have only to make our stay on planet Earth as pleasant as possible. And yet, the greatest saints and artists in Christian history have had little interest in proving Christ is Lord. Rather, the Lordship of Christ is a given, and they live and move in that belief. The Lordship of Christ is not the sum total of an equation, but the first line of a sprawling, unpredictable novel of spiritual liberty.

Whether or not we believe imitating the selfless works of Christ will do us any good, most American Christians approve of selflessness principally as it benefits the community. Recent broad cultural shifts away from corporate aesthetics and toward DIY aesthetics and localism have trickled down into American churches, and we now speak of "Church" and "church community" interchangeably. That which "fosters community," "builds community," and "furthers community" is sought for its own sake. "Community" is just insular enough to confer identity, but also democratic, fraternal, and sufficiently penetrable to be welcoming. The principal value of the Church is thus that of creating enclaves of likeminded individuals who weep and mourn together, and who are willing to bring soup to one another in the event of illness or bereavement. Likewise, any dogma which threatens the breadth of the community is viewed with suspicion or hostility. Giving offense is the greatest blasphemy, then, for nothing corrupts community like "a brother offended." The greatest ethereal blessing of the Resurrection is life eternal, but the greatest earthly boon of the Resurrection is simply the creation of an implausible fact, which, once accepted, graduates believers into a club of persons who aid one another economically and emotionally. However, the Christian stuck in solitary confinement or marooned alone on an island is bereft of any chance to help his friends, share the Gospel, or weep with those who weep. Neither are there any more icons to kiss, any more priests to hear confession, any more sacraments to receive in faith. He must confront God the way we all shall one day. He must meet God in his heart, in his very being.

In my fifth year as a teacher, I taught *The Consolation of Philosophy* by the sixth-entury Roman philosopher Boethius to a class of Medieval literature students, and I finally encountered a muscular answer to the question, "Why be good?" I read *The Consolation* at a time when I knew nothing at all. I read the book for the first time as I taught it, and it was the first work of philosophy I had ever really understood.

When in college I was required to read Michel Foucault's *The History of Sexuality* and found most of it incomprehensible gibberish, so when I thought of philosophy, I thought of a thing which was over my head. Were I to teach philosophy, I knew I would either need to first earn a doctorate, or else fake it. There was no time for the former, though I had long honed the ability to do the latter. However, with every lecture and every hour spent reading and discussing *The Consolation* in class, I found it shockingly easy to understand. Two weeks in, I realized I was not faking anything. I was learning, and the more I learned, the more my students learned, as well.

The summer before I taught *The Consolation*, my wife gave birth to our first child, a daughter, and I drew near to God in fear. In the first several days of Camilla's life, she slept more than I thought safe, and I often imagined her never waking up. Like many young fathers, I knew little about the health of an infant, and so her every sickness or possibility of sickness made me angry and terrified. I learned to speak to God in my heart, which I had not done since I was a child.

Having a child is a strange kind of existential consolation in itself, especially for those who have lived worthless lives and dread God's judgement. Camilla was my child, but her status as "my child" was merely a type of my status as God's child. She belonged to me, but only so that I might understand all men truly belong to God. A young father learns by trial and error, but also by intuition. I learned to pray intuitively. At night, Camilla screamed in fear and I held her and rocked her to sleep and would not put her down until she was at peace, and I said to God, "Do you see how I hold this child and will not let go? Someday I will die, and You must also hold me and not let go." This petition came naturally, easily, as though God had given me the work of rocking a screaming child to sleep just so I would have a path to this prayer.

Such preparation was necessary for teaching *The Consolation of Philosophy*, which is the most intuitive of books. When I say the book is intuitive, I mean it is rather easy to comprehend, and yet very hard to accept, for men often refuse to act according to intuition. We sin, it hurts us, we sin again. We suspect our friends are hurting themselves, yet we say and do nothing about it, preferring to watch our friends destroy themselves than risk embarrassment in confrontation. As a teacher, I have regularly seen parents act against their own better judgment and enable their children to destroy themselves. Self-hatred is dazzling, captivating, and asking other people to not be dazzling and captivating is embarrassing. If a man writes a beautiful song about how drugs destroyed his life, other men will listen to that song while they do drugs. Such is the nature of beauty.

The Consolation of Philosophy is a consolation of philosophy, although most people prefer the consolations of food, family, friends, liquor, gossip, pornography, video games, movies, drugs, sex, laughter, vanity, fanaticism, and amusement, which means *The Consolation* called me to abandon many of my favorite sanctuaries. All such earthly and lurid consolations were closed off from Boethius, who is both the author of *The Consolation*, but also the anti-hero of his own story. As with the historical Boethius, the character Boethius in *The Consolation* is a sixth-century Roman senator falsely accused of betraying his nation and condemned to die as a traitor. Imprisoned, morose, and feeling very sorry for himself, he is visited by Lady Philosophy, a personification of wisdom, or perhaps the feminine form of wisdom to whom Solomon often refers. Lady Philosophy comes to console, but also to accuse, teach, and rehabilitate. She not only wants Boethius to feel better, she wants him to be good, to become good, even if he only has a few days left to live and there is no one, apart from himself, whom his goodness will benefit. Everything is not alright, not because Boethius is imprisoned, but because Boethius' soul is postured against God.

Over the course of their one-hundred-page conversation in Boethius's jail cell, the Lady moves from giving practical and reasonable advice to challenging discourses on the divine nature. I found the early chapters of *The Consolation* familiar, even nostalgic, for parents often pacify the tears and tempers of older children with the "gentle medicines" of Lady Philosophy. However, as the book proceeds, the Lady's thought veers further and further from aphorism, maxim, and common sense. The final chapters of the work are cosmic, universal. Boethius's disappointment at how his life has turned out is gradually absorbed by increasing wonder at God's being. As I taught *The Consolation*, Boethius's candid admissions of his own failure to become a virtuous man cut me to the heart. Could I teach in the same way, I wondered? Could teaching be more a matter of confessing faults than modeling accomplishments?

At the same time, the first work of philosophy a man really understands also shapes and colors his interior life. A man is his body and a man is his soul—but a man's soul is also his companion. A man's soul is his friend, his interlocutor, his accuser, his witness. For most of my life, my soul had been nothing more than a dark room wherein ideas and relics could be haphazardly stored, but *The Consolation* illumined this room and allowed me to refine, adjust, and rearrange the private atmosphere of my being.

In Ecclesiastes, Solomon often introduces new lines of thought with, "Then I said in my heart," or "Then I said to myself." In teaching *The Consolation*, I recognized this separate heart from which Solomon spoke, the self to whom Solomon addressed his thoughts. The self to whom I spoke was a better and more austere version of myself who heard my thoughts with suspended judgement. It is this self who benefits from prayer, fasting, and almsgiving, but which is also beyond time and beyond change in the conventional sense of the word. This is a man's teleological self, his final self, a deferred self, the speculated and hoped-for self into which a man is, during this life, always progressing. It is this same self whom the prodigal son discovers while languishing amidst the filth of pigs, for the epiphany which brings the destitute boy home begins with him "coming to himself" (Luke 15:17). Every man must come to this self in order to beg forgiveness, to imagine forgiveness possible, to imagine himself virtuous. *The Consolation* introduced me to this self, dressed him in a finer set of clothes, and arranged a table and chairs where we could sit and converse. The man who listens to this other person becomes a "spiritual man," as St. Paul says.

So much talk of "the self" is apt to disturb many Christians who have been taught that community and "others" are all that matter. However, we lack a refined ability to distinguish between self-awareness and self-obsession, which sound similar, yet are truly opposites. St. Paul does not teach that a man should "not think of himself," but that he should "not think of himself more highly than he ought" (Rom. 12:3). A man's recognition of his separate heart, his austere and deferred self, is the beginning of his self-effacement, his quietude, his teachable spirit. If the self were a problem, the prodigal son's salvation would not begin with his discovery of the self, but his rejection of it. The only self-improvement which saves is the self-eschewing described by St. John the Baptist, who sees Christ and says, "He must increase, but I must decrease" (John 3:30). In truth, this separate heart is not so much a self as it is the revelation of the omnipresent God.

The man who has self-awareness is able to see himself as a character in a story, though not the main character. He is not bound to his own perspective of the world, but views his words and actions from a third-person distance and has the power to critique himself with impartiality. The teacher who desperately longs for the approval of his students and is willing to sacrifice his dignity in order to win the passing respect of ersatz rebels—such a man obviously lacks self-awareness, for he does not know the contempt with which readers would regard the novel of his life. The mother who insists her fourteen-year-old son does not know what sex is similarly lacks self-awareness. She does not know the audience is laughing at her. The man with self-awareness cultivates a second self with which to investigate the actions of his first self, and this second self maintains average opinions, standard prejudices, and ordinary tastes. And yet, in *The Consolation*, Lady Philosophy teaches Boethius to reach for something beyond self-awareness, and by the end of the book, Boethius is not merely content to come off as winsome, charming, or any of the qualities that make for a decent coworker, or which win sympathy in a Jane Austen novel or a Richard Curtis film. Rather, Boethius reaches for the aerial perspective of that great cloud of witnesses which has passed from this world and into the next life, where earthly glory, amusement, power, and pleasure largely prove to have been a waste of time.

Chapter by chapter, I was moved by the way Boethius the author confessed his faults and ignorance through Boethius the character. Boethius was content that much of his life had been a waste, and in his final moments before shuffling off this mortal coil, he used the figure of Lady Philosophy as a separate heart to investigate his own corrupt heart. He offered no genuine self-defense, but condemned himself as a man who had lived for the praise of men. And yet, by the final page, I could believe Boethius had nearly written himself into the wise figure of Lady Philosophy. He had left behind his desire for earthly, sensual consolations, and stepped into a better self. He had decreased, and Christ had increased. He no longer lived, but Christ lived within. I accepted Boethius's offer to condemn myself, and began proving Lady Philosophy's claims about the good life true by telling of my own moral failures and what unhappiness they attended.

There is no good apart from Christ.

By the time I finished *The Consolation* for the first time, I understood that every great work of literature could be used as instruction in virtue. *The Consolation* was not unique. All great authors invariably offer a vision of the more noble life to which they long to ascend and invite their readers along as disciples and fellow pilgrims. What is more, any book could be taught like *The Consolation*. The teacher might vindicate the text by confessing his own failure to live up to the moral vision elucidated by the author. As the school year continued, I found myself depending on this same theory when lecturing on other books and other subjects. I found my confessions were best attended by a homiletic tone, which improved into a sermonic mood. I began pacing around the classroom as I taught, upbraiding, thundering, whispering, and pleading. From that point forward, everything I have done in the classroom has been a footnote referencing my first encounter with Boethius.

I should unapologetically state up front that I play fast and loose with every book I teach, which means I have never met a good story which is too far from the subject at hand. An overdependence on grammatical and historical methods of interpreting the Bible has spooked modern Christians into believing a good interpretation uses all the pieces of the original. However, a text is not a pile of blocks, and an interpretation is not the mere rearrangement of those blocks into a different pattern. Any interpretation which accounts for everything in the original text is simply not worth doing, for it treats words as mere material, not as incarnations of spirit. The writers of the New Testament are often at pains to show Christ as a second Adam, second Moses, second Solomon, and the fact that all the pieces of the Old Testament heroes cannot be used in their Messianic fulfillment did not deter the Gospel writers from furiously drawing connections. The relationship between a text and its sound interpretation is not like the relationship between a Lego car and a Lego castle, each made of the same 812 blocks. Rather, text and interpretation are like father and son, cello and cello suite, milk and cheese.

The claim that a good teacher labors to pass down "the spirit" of a text may strike readers as subjective and flimsy, the same kind of sentimental foolishness which similarly demands trophies be given out for nineteenth place. We roll our eyes at "the spirit of cooking" or "the spirit of fashion," as though these phrases were the typical refuges of people too stupid to master actual food and actual fabric. On the contrary, I sat through scores of classes in high school and college wherein the material of the text was the only thing taught, the only thing tested, and I can recall nothing of these classes but the banal feeling which attended their completion. I have memorized lists of kings, lists of elements, lists of theories, and I have taken reams of tests wherein I was asked to recapitulate plots of novels and sequences of arguments. The mediocre teacher explains the themes of the book, the book is read, and then the teacher asks once again, "What are the themes of this book?" On a whim, the teacher might require students to prooftext their answers on the final, and the only satisfaction the student gains from such tests is the knowledge that any test which is dull to take is twice as dull to grade. I have taken assessments wherein a teacher had selected quotes from a dozen characters in the book, demanded the students identify which character had said what, then explain the significance of the quote—and, what surpasses the imagination, the teacher required students to do this without the use of their books. All such tests reject the "spirit of the text" in favor of the textual material, by which I mean the grammar, vocabulary, author's biography, exact sequence of the plot, demographics of the characters, and so forth. Such information is quickly and naturally jettisoned by the mind as superfluous once the final exam is taken, but anything worth memorizing is worth memorizing by repetition, over the course of weeks, by way of daily recitation. Precious little of what I was asked to learn in high school or college was presented as having inherent value, but grades were nothing more than bartering chips which could be traded up for more desirable goods later, like scholarships or higher paying jobs.*

The good teacher must recognize the sobering fact that, by the start of sophomore year, students recall almost none of the content they studied freshman year. Material slips from the mind with unsettling ease. Readers of this book might ask themselves how much high school algebra they recall, what they remember about the War of 1812, or whether they can explain the difference between a mitochondria and an organelle. The average reader, I wager, remembers nothing about these matters, yet passed a test on them long ago. The good teacher must give his students something which will survive the mind's inevitable loss of the material.

After the literature student has forgotten the names of the characters in *Frankenstein*, what will remain? After the history student has forgotten who led the New Model Army, what will linger in the imagination? The good teacher sees beyond the pretense of his students "mastering" *Paradise Lost* in a single read and aims, rather, to indelibly watermark the student's soul with great literature. The good teacher stores his most precious teaching in the soul of the student, where thieves cannot break in and steal. The good teacher inspires desire for God in his students, and calls them to yearn for Beauty and strive for piety and holiness and virtue. The good teacher tells his students, "If you see me as I am being taken from you, you will receive a double portion of my spirit," for he can offer his students nothing greater. The student trains his eye on the teacher and will look at nothing else, the teacher trains his eye on Goodness and will look at nothing else. Slowly, the student comprehends the paradox, then the teacher is gone and the student will look only at

---

* Many thanks to Brian Williams for his remarkable lecture at the 2017 Alcuin Retreat in which he suggested the "trading up" analogy.

God—but first the student must learn what kind of devotion Goodness requires. These are my interests in *The Consolation*, or any great book in the Western canon, for that matter, and my reading and lecturing on *The Consolation* are born of these ends. I will gaze at Boethius and not look away, for Boethius was a friend of God and I do not know God without the help of His friends.

Given such designs, my time teaching *The Consolation* is unevenly distributed between its pages. *The Consolation of Philosophy* is divided into five books, though I devote more time to the first three books than the latter two. The first three books are far more suited to Americans, to teenagers, and to the middle-class affairs of myself and most of my students. In the first three books, Boethius and Lady Philosophy discuss luck, work, death, and all the petty amusements that make the lives of petty men worth living. A barrage of subjects is covered, none of which will strike readers as foreign or esoteric. However, in the final two books of *The Consolation*, Boethius presses Lady Philosophy for an explanation of evil, and Lady Philosophy delves into difficult teachings on human freedom and metaphysics. The final two books are by no means too difficult for high school students to understand, yet there are far fewer homilies to be preached on these passages. Rather, Lady Philosophy makes an ever more direct point about God's relationship with man which exonerates God of evil and shifts a profound moral weight onto man.

It was not my goal to write an academic commentary on *The Consolation of Philosophy*, for the book you now hold was not intended to fill the bibliographies of journals on medieval literature." Rather, this book is for classical educators, for parents of students in classical schools, but also for anyone dissatisfied with the school their child currently attends. This book is even for disgruntled students who feel school—be it a public school, classical school, private school, or home school—is basically a waste of time. This book is for good students and for bad students, for it was written by a bad student who accidentally became a teacher. There are few footnotes, and I have not engaged with many scholarly readings of Boethius. Rather, this book is for anyone in education who is in over their head—teachers and students and administration alike. The strategies I employ in teaching virtue through classic texts owe entirely to the fact that I was a terrible, slothful student in high school, but I simply cannot say anything about *The Consolation* or the pedagogical arts until I describe the curious path which took me from disinterested student to zealous teacher.

"I want you to see how true respect cannot be obtained through the insubstantial honours of high office . . ."

- Lady Philosophy, 3.4 (p. 55)

Over the first several chapters of *The Consolation*, readers find that former Roman senator Boethius has been convicted of treason and sent into exile where he awaits execution. While imprisoned, Boethius feels a sharp sting in his loss of a high and respected office, and yet Lady Philosophy, his interlocutor and tutor, insists that in losing his position, he has not lost anything of real value.

No one, she says, becomes good or happy simply in being elected or taking the throne. "More often than removing wickedness, high office brings it to light" (p. 54), the Lady argues. High office is an effect of good fortune, not a quality inherent in the man who occupies the office. Even if power could make men happy, power can yet be lost, and so power becomes yet another thing a man must worry about losing. "What is this power, then, which cannot banish the nagging of worry or avoid the pin-prick of fear? Kings would like to live free from worry, but they can't" (p 56). The more power a man has, the more he fears to lose. So what is the man thrown into a position of power to do? Are kings fated for anxious lives? Are princes bound for unhappiness? Christ gives peace, but "not as the world gives," which means that Christ also gives laws but "not as the world gives." Christ chides the Gentiles, who lord their power over the little people (Matt. 20:25), but commands His disciples to seek out greatness by serving others. To satisfy both the cautions of Lady Philosophy and the commands of Christ, the man who comes into authority and power should not use his position to cloak his vices, neither should he treat his position as an icon of his own virtue. Rather, authority should be physically and spiritually spent up. So far as my own career is concerned, I count myself blessed by God to have learned this lesson quite early. Any success I have enjoyed as an educator entirely derives from an early willingness to use my own life as a cautionary tale for others.

My present work as a classical educator comes as something of a surprise to my former instructors, many of whom I still talk to. Given the disappointment I inspired in my own teachers, was choosing teaching as a career an act of self-loathing? Or penance, perhaps? However, it is only by a stroke of good luck that I became a teacher. It had nothing to do with merit, and certainly nothing to do with virtue.

The only academic virtue I possessed in high school was an interest and ability to imitate the way adults spoke. I did not read much as a child, nor was I required to read, although from the time I was five or six, I was intrigued by the cadences, grammar, and construction of mature conversations. Over time, this interest blossomed into an ability to write clearly, for as I wrote, I heard what I wrote, and when I heard what I wrote, I heard a stately, dignified voice speaking my words in rich, round tones. When my words were unworthy of the voice speaking them, I changed them until they fit. All the same, I was not a reader and neither was I humble, and so regardless of the rhetorical and stylistic flourishes at my disposal, most of what I had to say was ephemeral and vain. My talent for writing was occasionally remarked upon by teachers, although I was one of those young men who is unfortunately told, "You are very smart, but you could be accomplishing so much more if you were diligent..." I took this to mean that I could coast into adulthood. By carrying on the same slothful and lackadaisical trajectory, I was more or less guaranteed an 80 percent share of whatever success had come to my parents. If I wanted to make a name for myself, or if I wanted to make more money than my father, I could always apply myself; however, should I never get bitten by the bug of ambition, a life of basic comfort was nonetheless in the cards for me.

I held such beliefs when I began college at the University of Idaho in the fall of 1999, and because I had no respect for the institution, I fared poorly and dropped out less than six weeks after my first day of class. For the next several years, I maintained a miserable job at a market research firm, wrote quite a bit, started and attended a few writing clubs, endured more than twenty thousand miles on Greyhound busses, briefly worked at an illegal casino, went back to school once again, dropped out once again, and finally moved to Chicago where I lived with a friend for nine months, working in the front office of a private Christian school on the south side of the city. Shortly before I left for Chicago, I stopped by my old school and spoke with my former British literature teacher, a woman with a deserved reputation as a sage, and the kind of curious, gatekeeping soul with whom it is lucky to speak with before a major undertaking. We conversed briefly, though I remember little of what she told me aside from a little news about her daughter, who was lonely and living in Providence, Rhode Island. "You should write her," she suggested, and gave me her email address. I arrived in Chicago in early July, we began corresponding a month later, and at Thanksgiving I took a bus to see her. By the same time the following year, we had both moved back to the Pacific Northwest and Paula had agreed to marry me.

Her parents consented to the marriage provided I finish college, though they were willing to take my word. When we married in March of 2006, I still needed more than thirty credits to graduate. Around the time I was re-enrolling in college, I chanced upon an old acquaintance from a writing club I formerly attended. The fellow was a solid twenty years older than myself (I had been the only person in the club younger than tweny-five) and all the rest of the members were similarly former teachers and fathers of grown children. He told me he was on the board of a small private school which had lately opened, and that the school was looking for a writing teacher. Recalling me as a decent writer, he asked if I was interested. The job paid little, but required little. On a lark, I took it.

Of course, I knew nothing of teaching, and so far as academics were concerned, I was a career slacker. Composition was the only marketable skill I possessed. The degree in English which I was working toward would be of little value in the job market, and, when anyone inquired I was still in the habit of saying, "I would like to be a writer someday," although I mostly hoped nobody would ask. Looking back now, I have not a blessed clue why Paula agreed to marry me. In my first year teaching, I was given a single composition class. After enjoying a little success with that, the following year I was asked to teach an English class, as well, and in my third year I was additionally put in charge of a world history class. While I am given to hyperbole, it would not be too much to say this history class turned my life around.

The textbook I was given to use was an Abeka world history book. The classes met but once a week, and for the remainder of the week students were in a guided study hall, though their labors were largely self-directed. I assigned massive chunks of the book every week, and when we met to discuss, the class would gloss hundreds of years of history. The further we progressed in the text, the less I liked it. Nearly any history book attempting to go from the Garden of Eden to Mikhail Gorbachev in four hundred heavily illustrated pages will make for dry reading, for history must be reduced to a sequence of laws and wars, and even the laws and wars are reduced to names and dates. The reader is lucky to find more than a sentence devoted to Bach or Shakespeare. My disinterest in the book turned to disgust, however, when we reached the chapters on the Middle Ages and I came across a passage which suggested the entire medieval era (a thousand years of history which comprised numerous languages and cultures) was brutal, violent, and that medieval men and women alike were filthy, uncultured, and typically drunk.

In my third year as a teacher, I was nonetheless the same slacker I had been back in high school, and yet I still found the Abeka account of the Middle Ages deeply problematic. The Middle Ages had lasted for nearly a thousand years, and had every inhabitant of Europe been drunk for a millennium? But who built Notre Dame? Winos? And what filthy thug was it who conceived of the rose window in the Chartres cathedral? The book was risible, farcical. I was not a student of history, but I had written more than one thousand pages of fiction, and I understood the good author must respect and love his creations if he wants his reader to do the same. Intuitively, I knew the good historian must love his subject, as well, although the evangelical authors of *History of the World in Christian Perspective* made little effort to veil a brazen contempt for the Catholic Church. I began doing a good deal of research on my own, consulting primary sources, and when class met to discuss our reading, I spent the whole hour debunking all the specious claims made in the homework. Vindicating Western history as a reasonable story was not merely thrilling, but deeply satisfying.

By this time, I was also in my second year of marriage. Paula was the primary wage-earner, I was on the verge of earning my diploma, and still no possible career had opened up before me. A friend who lived in Florida had been teaching at a classical Christian school for several years, and when I described for him my heroic battles against Abeka ignorance, he said, "I could get you a job at the school where I teach." I interviewed. I graduated college. My wife and I sold everything which wouldn't fit in a 1998 Toyota Corolla, drove to Florida, and started life anew.

The problem remained, though: I knew basically nothing. My new job was unlike my old job in that I had now been hired to teach great books. *History of the World in a Christian Perspective* was such a profoundly incompetent work of propaganda, a single hour spent on Wikipedia could give a man sufficient ammunition to mow down every sentence in the book. In my new position, though, I would be teaching Edmund Burke, Jean-Jacques Rousseau, and the same ancient literature which I bypassed with CliffsNotes back in high school. To be blunt, I had talked a good game to get the job, but I was entirely unprepared to teach anything more venerable than *Rolling Stone* magazine. I realized this at the time, though, and I was well-served by the embarrassing recognition that I was unqualified for the work of teaching great books. From the point I took the lectern, I quit pretending. I claimed no power over the books I taught. I was in no position to judge them, to gerrymander true statements from false, or to divulge the worldview of the author and expose his school of thought as fraud. I introduced each book to my students the way a man introduces someone he has just met at a party. Every book had to be taught page by page. Swamped, I could not even stay a chapter ahead of my students. I was often surprised by words I read aloud in class, the directions in which philosophical arguments turned, and the curious plot twists of novels.

A teacher is either working to give students power over the text, or he is showing students how to enthrone the book in their hearts. The teacher who gives students power over the text wants the students to draw a very particular set of conclusions about a book, namely that the book is right or wrong. He tells them the text is good or bad before beginning to teach it, clearly elucidates the worldview of the author in a series of propositional statements on the board, like "Romantics believe nature is good," and then uses the text to vindicate the claim, "*Frankenstein* is a work of Romanticism." Having reduced *Frankenstein* to a work of Romanticism, Romanticism can then be judged as valid or invalid after a hasty comparison with a few perspicuous verses from Paul's letters. Given that very few books written in the last five centuries forthrightly declare, "Jesus is Lord," the teacher who wants to give his students power over great works of literature must be in the habit of declaring classic texts "wrong." The only "right books" he teaches are less than twenty years old, published by Crossway or InterVarsity Press, and just happen to be personal favorites of the theology teacher.

Some would say that the only point in teaching wrong books is to "plunder the Egyptians." Wrong books are rife with philosophical errors, however, we can learn effective rhetoric, elegant style, and hone our ability to craft a well-turned phrase by reading them. The empowering teacher turns the reading of old books into a game, a physical struggle, wherein Shelley or Rousseau or Homer is attempting to shoot intellectual hockey pucks into the net of our minds, and the careful reader is a goalie whose task is to deflect them. The best kind of reader, then, gains nothing new in the reading of a classic text, but merely has his beliefs strengthened, solidified. When finished with a text, the student is given a test wherein he exposes the dogmas of the author as unbiblical or illogical or unrepublican. Such tests often require the student to do little more than prooftext the teacher's introduction of the book, and feature challenges like, "Use three passages in *Frankenstein* to show Shelley's worship of nature." The high marks a student receives on such a test prove he has mastered the text, beaten the book at its own game, outmaneuvered it, defied ideas which have stood the test of time. The student relishes a feeling of authority over the text and the teacher enjoys the thrill of telling himself his pupils, mere children, have overcome books which are yet labored over by doctors of philosophy at prestigious universities.

Even to teach a classic text in this truncated manner, a modicum of knowledge about the book and of philosophical systems is required; however, when I began teaching classic texts, I could not claim to have ever read a classic book all on my own. Nihilism, materialism, and Gnosticism were terms I had heard, but about which I had no real knowledge. If the teacher knows nothing of Romanticism, there is little point in claiming "*Frankenstein* is a work of Romanticism" while handing out copies of the text. Most of my time in class was spent reading our texts out loud, then blandly polling the class, "So what do you think? Thoughts?" Outside of class, I feverishly studied and read as many commentaries on the curriculum and secondary sources as I could find, but none of this was sufficient to overcome the helpless feeling which haunted me whenever I opened a book in class. Then I taught *The Consolation of Philosophy*, and my whole approach to teaching was upended.

As the year passed, I slowly discovered that every book I taught was ultimately interested in the question, "What does it mean to be a good human being?" Every great author made claims about how a man should live, how he should treat his brothers, what service he owed to God. All human beings— even adolescent human beings who are otherwise wholly captivated by sensual folly— are still readily intrigued by conversations about right and wrong. Because I was essentially uneducated, the only supplemental material I could bring to bear on the text was my own life, and so I read to my students and waited for the author to make a claim about the good life, then I vindicated that claim with a story drawn from my own experiences. As I had done little good in my life, most of the stories I told were about my own moral and spiritual failures, and the embarrassment and sorrow solicited in sin.

Stories of my own failures were exactly what my students needed to hear.

CHAPTER TWO

Death as a
Practical Problem

> **"Surely the severity of Fortune's attack on me needs
> no further mention; it is self evident . . ."**
>
> **- Boethius, 1.4 (p. 9)**

When Lady Philosophy encounters Boethius in the early chapters of *The Consolation*, he has lost his wife and nation and power and wealth and he wants to die, so sick is he over these losses. Philosophy knows, however, that the loss of his body will not remove these appetites from his soul. Philosophy takes a practical approach to death.

A man going on a hike may take whatever will fit in a backpack. He is free to take dry socks, a sleeping bag, and a compass, but he can also take a disco ball and a bucket of light bulbs if he so chooses. The former items will be of use to him, the latter items will not. The question of what to take on a hike is eminently practical, though, and not existential. In like manner, Boethius can take his desire for his wife, his home, and his power when he goes to meet God, but these desires are not specifically Christian. If Boethius goes to meet God and there is nothing he wants which only God can give, God will send him out of His presence to a place where Boethius can secure the things he wants.

For eight years in a row now, I have become sick over the course of

the summer and feared for my life. When I am sick, I find it very easy
to be good and resist temptation. Sickness makes monks of us all, even
if only for a time. We cannot eat so much as we would like, sleeping
becomes difficult, and we look forward with trepidation to our passage
into the next life. Desire fails. No one understands popular culture so
clearly as the man in the waiting room who shortly expects a diagnosis
of cancer, but who is, for the moment, flipping through *US Weekly*. "All
is vanity," he mutters with unfeigned disgust.

The kinds of sickness I suffer from during the summer are typically
vague, uncertain. A heaviness or feeling of weightlessness suddenly in
my kidneys or liver. An irregular heartbeat, or a fast heartbeat. Nau-
sea, numbness in the hands or feet. The symptoms of an ulcer and the
symptoms of pancreatic cancer overlap enough to confuse the two, at
least for the layman, although the former is an inconvenience and the
latter often a hasty death sentence. When I am sick, I find myself more
easily capable of overcoming all the standard temptations I typically
fall to. The first time I understood "the terror of the Lord" (2 Cor. 5:11)
St. Paul references was the first summer I became ill. My heart began
to skip beats several times a day, and a mysterious pain near my heart
would come and go, although I often had difficulty saying for certain
where exactly the pain was. One night, I had run out on an errand, and
while at the store my heart skipped a beat, then another beat, and just a
moment later, another. Let us set aside exactly how worried I ought to
have been over such irregularities, for in truth, I was quickly becoming
convinced death was only days away.

When I returned to my car for a short drive home, two CDs sat in the
passenger's side seat: a recording of Rachmaninoff's "All-Night Vigil"
and New Order's *Power, Corruption & Lies*. While this would prove a
fairly mundane choice for most people, with the prospect of death on
the horizon, the decision suddenly seemed monumental. I asked myself,
"Which one of these pieces of music is more likely to be of value to me
when I die?" Death no longer seemed an existential problem, but a prac-

tical problem which could be approached with common sense. I was not one who ever objected to classical music, and I could be brought to enjoy a work of Debussy or Mozart if someone else in the house was determined to listened to it. However, classical music was not something to which I felt any ready, natural inclination. On the other hand, I had been a committed devotee of pop music since I was twelve. Popular music was easy to like, but classical music difficult, so when I say that death seemed a practical problem, I mean that, sitting in the car that evening, I tried to imagine New Order's *Power, Corruption & Lies* possibly having any value for me after I died. I asked myself whether it was within the realm of my wildest imagination that, after my soul departed my body and was somewhere between this earth and the final judgment, there might be some condition where it would prove valuable to have listened to New Order's 1983 synth pop classic. I could imagine no such condition, though. I should note that I make no claim to special knowledge of what happens to a man after he dies, and the questions I was asking in the car that night were more a matter of suspicion and intuition not dogma. And yet when I asked myself whether I could imagine a better acquaintance with Rachmaninoff's "All-Night Vigil" might do me some service upon my death, the answer was, "Perhaps." I could *imagine* it. The question became a guiding light which often directed my actions over the course of that summer.

Unfortunately, however, my health improved when the school year began.

Another summer I suffered a peculiar bout of food poisoning in which my desire to eat disappeared, followed by my desire for sex, then my want for alcohol, then music, then amusement of any kind. It was the first time in my life in which all of these desires had simultaneously vacated my soul. I was disoriented. The average sick American has earned the right to lay in bed and watch television, but I had no want of television. Amusement seemed absurd. What is more, my desire for food and drink was not simply being overwhelmed by other desires.

During other bouts of intense physical illness, I have recognized all the standard desires for sensual things yet exist within me, but have been covered over with greater desires for the rest and moderation necessary to restore a body to health. But to suddenly lose all these desires completely was bewildering. I dropped little stones into the well of my spirit, and no desire for physical pleasure echoed back. I felt adrift. I realized that even when I had not been actively contemplating sensual pleasure or planning how I might get it, I had nonetheless been ruminating on it, mulling it over in the back of my mind. Monks often employ this same part of their minds for prayer, but I used it to think about Sofia Coppola movies and brunch.

During the first several days of the ordeal, a former student suffered the untimely and unforeseeable loss of her father in a tragic accident. She posted a photo of herself on Facebook, perhaps when she was only two years old, giving her father a kiss. Her eyes were closed in the picture and she held a stuffed duck. A look of utter delight illumined her face. I spent nearly a week meditating on the photo, sometimes weeping. I had not seen or spoken with the former student in years, and yet the photo nourished my soul in way no piece of music or film or book had accomplished in years. These weeks of sickness seemed timeless, not because they dragged on, but because I could not understand why I did not always live without desire, and because I could not fathom returning to the same sensual desires that typically governed my life.

Unfortunately, however, my health once again improved.

To consider death as a practical problem is to acknowledge that when time finally separates our bodies from our souls, we will nonetheless be ourselves. Our souls do not possess a separate personhood when we die. All the thoughts and desires a man develops while living are yet with him when he is dead. Sensual desires are not sloughed off simply because the body is sloughed off. It is not as though a painter who suddenly loses the use of his hands also suddenly loses his desire to paint. The athlete who suddenly loses the use of his legs does not also suddenly lose his passion for running. The art critic who goes blind at the age of fifty does not also summarily jettison his desire to gaze at art and contemplate its value. Death is very much like the painter who loses his hands, or the athlete who loses his legs, or the art critic who loses his eyes, however, in death we do not merely lose one or two of our members, but all of them. If the body has not been used to serve the soul, death will involve the loss of all that made life worth living. If a man's whole identity is bound up in the use of his body, death will not be unpleasant, but near annihilation of personhood. Christians do not believe that the body is worthless. Christians believe that the body is good, however, they also traditionally hold that the soul is more important than the body. The body is ephemeral, the soul is eternal. It is better to enter Heaven maimed than go to Hell with your body intact (Matt. 18:8). We should not fear them who can destroy the body, but Him who can throw body and soul into Hell (Matt. 10:28).

In the parable of Lazarus and the rich man, both titular figures die and go off to their respective rewards. While in Hades, the rich man makes a strange request. "Father Abraham, have mercy on me, and send Lazarus that he may dip the tip of his finger in water and cool my tongue; for I am tormented in this flame" (Luke 16:24). If the parable has ever seemed odd, and yet the reader cannot exactly say why, perhaps it has something to do with the fact that dead men do not have tongues. While the dead no longer have use of their tongues, they nonetheless carry the appetites of the body with them into the grave. The man whose life revolves around gratifying sexual wants takes those sexual wants with him to the grave, though he no longer has his body or the bodies of others with which to spend his lust. The man with a desire for booze no longer has a cerebral cortex to assault once he dies. Neither has a man eyes to watch a film, fingers to play games, or a stomach for food.

This is not how the typical American Christian has come to think of the grave, though. In the South, a great many billboards depict a flatlining electrocardiogram with the message, "After you die, you will meet

God." While the average atheist doubts the words "meet God" in this maxim, the average Christian doubts the word "you." He finds it hard to believe that he himself will go to meet God, but that some avatar of himself or some idealized proxy of himself will go to meet God. The word "you" scarcely refers to any real person, but an abstract personage who shares none of the same wants, desires, or knowledge that a man has while alive. He reasons like a gnostic for whom the body is nothing more than a prison. Having escaped this prison, he will become his real and good self. While "present in the body," he has a profound desire for sex, liquor, and amusement, but such desires are bound up in the body, and once the body is excreted, all such desire will suddenly vanish.

The parable of Lazarus and the rich man suggests something far different, though. "Going to be with God" is a good bit like "going to the store." When a man is hungry he goes to the store. He does not send some ideal version of himself to the store. He does not send an icon of himself to the store. Rather, he himself gets in the car. He, with all his desires, foibles, virtues, idiosyncrasies, proclivities. When he arrives at the store, he walks around shopping. *He* shops. He shops with all his thoughts and memories and hopes. Likewise, when a man dies and goes to be with God, he goes to be with God. It is not that he sends some perfect and flawless emissary of himself. He goes himself to receive "the things done in the body," whether good or bad.

"No man is rich who shakes and groans
Convinced that he needs more."
- Lady Philosophy, 2.2 (p. 26)

"... so far from being able to remove want,
riches create a want of their own ..."
- Lady Philosophy, 3.3 (p. 53)

The Lady is often at pains to prove that money cannot buy happiness, but that it can buy unhappiness. A man cannot control his luck or his situation forever, but he can control his desires. The only difference between a blessing and a curse is whether a man gives thanks or not. The things he blesses bless him back. The things he damns damn him in return. Boethius laments the untimely loss of his money and his home, and yet, on the day Boethius was born, Fate decreed the ultimate loss of these things. The only way to escape the inevitable pain of death is to practice dying long in advance. If you die before you die then you won't die when you die, reads the well-known inscription on the gateway to an Orthodox monastery on Mount Athos.

"Money cannot buy happiness" is often mistakenly interpreted to mean, "Money cannot buy pleasure," and money can most certainly buy pleasure. However, money cannot remove want, and neither can cash make a man self-sufficient. Money can satisfy want, but the satisfaction of want and the removal of want are two different things. Satisfied wants invariably come back.

"Everyone who drinks of this water will be thirsty again," (John 4:13) says Christ, and the same is true of food. The man who eats food, though briefly satiated, will hunger again. The man who takes his wife to bed will desire her again the following night. The sad woman who purchases a purse to cheer herself up will eventually become melancholy once again. The tired man may sleep his fill, though he will need rest again just hours later. Most Americans do not know how many wants they have, and neither do they understand the profound depth of those wants, simply because most of their wants are daily, unproblematically fulfilled.

When we speak of "satisfaction," we speak relatively. Every claim to satisfaction is attended by a silent "for the time being." Because nothing earthly can ultimately satisfy a man, Solomon finds the world a tiresome place. "All things are full of weariness; a man cannot utter it; the eye is not satisfied with seeing, nor the ear filled with hearing . . . what has been done is what will be done" (Ecc. 1:8-9). The eye has never seen enough, the ear has never heard enough, the mouth has never consumed enough. No food is so good as to end a man's desire. No bread is delicious enough that the man who eats it declares, "I will never desire bread again." No painting is so beautiful that the woman beholding it says, "My enjoyment of paintings has come to an end. I no longer need art." The more excellent the thing enjoyed, the more acute the desire for that thing. Saying such things is one thing, believing them is another, but acting on them is something quite alien to the natural mind.

I have always been in love. My first crush came in second grade, and since then, not a day of my life has passed wherein I was not romantically interested in someone. However, romantic intrigue occupied only a small corner of my imagination until I discovered pop music when I was fourteen. I had lately gone from being homeschooled to attending a private Christian school, and at this private school, everyone listened to the radio. One night, out of curiosity, I scanned a radio dial until I found "Two Princes" by The Spin Doctors playing on a Top 40 station. As Semele was annihilated before the transfigured Zeus, so my soul was absorbed into the zeitgeist. Popular music is little more than the worship of Romance and so my newly discovered devotion to popular music quickly glorified my casual interest with love into a bona fide cult.

In school, I learned that the primary value of Christianity was that it offered a proper worldview with which I could assess the truth of philosophical claims and vindicate the substance of arguments. However, the idea that the world was primarily a place to be viewed, seen, judged, vindicated, or condemned simply failed to arrest my imagination. I did not want to view the world, I wanted to be in the world, to be of the world, to devour the world and be devoured by the world in return. I wanted to enjoy the world the way Annie Dillard enjoyed Tinker Creek. I wanted to enjoy the world the way General Löwenhielm enjoyed wine in *Babette's Feast*, the way St. Francis enjoyed poverty, the way Steven Spielberg enjoyed innocence. When I refer to "the world," I mean both popular culture and romantic love, for all the music and films I gave myself over to were hymns to love and epics of love. Romantic love was the apex of all human experience, the highest calling of the human heart, and neither the Iliad nor Silas Marner excited feelings of longing, passion, desire, despair, or melancholy quite like Radiohead's "Creep." I worshipped Romance as a god. My worship was not of the limp modern variety, wherein a man must weekly gin up the humility to pretend to be sixteen again for Jesus. My worship of Romance was monastic, Roman Catholic, pagan, Babylonian, Franciscan, desperate, pathetic, austere, and dignified. I memorized the lyrics to Oasis songs and Smashing Pumpkins songs the way Orthodox monks memorize the Psalter, through sheer repetition. I bought massive studio headphones and listened to *OK Computer* with the volume turned all the way up while palming the speakers deeper into my head, as though the immaterial music was also a physical reality—as though the lyrics were bread and my ears were suppliant mouths.

As the widow piously gave her two pennies to the temple, I spent all my money on music. When I was a freshman, my father gave me a generous ten dollars a week for performing a few chores. Given the cost of music in the 1990s, my allowance afforded me two new CDs a month, provided I spent my money on nothing else. Purchasing a new CD was usually something of a gamble, then, for these were the days when there was no way of listening to an album before buying it, and one often heard friends sadly report that an album lately purchased "only had one good song on it." I was very judicious in my purchases, though, and spent hours reading reviews in *Rolling Stone*, *Spin*, *Q*, and *Uncut* before committing to anything. On the rare occasion the reviews steered me wrong, I was stuck with what I had bought and made an effort to learn to like it.

By the time I graduated high school, I viewed my record collection as an avatar of my soul, an extension of my mind, an icon of what I loved and how I loved, how I wanted to love and (most importantly) how I wanted to be loved. It was a statement about who I was, what I believed, where my loyalties were. Had a stranger asked me, "What kind of person are you?" I would have taken that stranger to my CD racks. Were a stranger to ask me the same question today, I would probably show him my children. As for my collection of CDs, I could refine such a soul, edit it, or purge it. On one occasion, I sold my entire CD collection for cash so I could buy a bus ticket and go to be with the first real girlfriend I ever had. At the time, this struck me as an entirely appropriate sacrifice, for the purpose of popular music had always been access to Romantic sentiment; selling my CD collection for cash to be with a woman was tantamount to Zwingli sublimely taking a bite out of a Bible. The signifier transformed into the sign itself. Religious epiphanies have also resulted in costly music reformations. The day after I saw *The Royal Tenenbaums*, I sold around $1,200 worth of techno records for around $150 and purchased albums by The Rolling Stones, The Velvet Underground, and Jeff Buckley. As of today, I own around one thousand CDs, however, over the course of my life, I would wager I have owned between ten thousand and fifteen thousand CDs. This odd fact neatly coincides with the fact that I am a very movable man; at the age of thirty-six, I have been a member of a Southern Baptist church, an OPC church, a CREC church, as well as non-denominational Bible churches, international churches, military chapels, and non-Trinitarian cults. I have never kept a single mailing residence for longer than five years. Personal upheavals are betokened by musical upheavals, although popular music has proven to have such idolatrous power over my soul, it might be more fitting to say musical upheavals are betokened by personal upheavals.

Before I discovered the Bible, popular music was for me a kind of Old Testament, or else I loved popular music the way the Jews were commanded to love the words of God. In my adolescence, popular music was sacred and bore witness to something transcendent. Pop music was priestly, a bridge between what is common and what is holy. I did not merely listen to popular music. I meditated on it. I intuited that holy things could not be taken at face value, and imposed a quadriga upon the paeans to Aphrodite and Eros I heard on the radio. In the same way St. Augustine's prose is inundated with Scriptural phrases and allusions, I could not speak without invoking films and songs. I fixed the words of Thom Yorke in my heart and mind, I tied them as symbols on my hands and bound them on my forehead. I discussed them with my friends, talked about them at the lunch table, and whispered them to myself when I walked home from school. I repeated them before falling asleep every night and every morning when I woke. I wrote them on the walls of my room, on my locker door, and between the notes I took in history class. The most profound kind of maturity a man could reach was not intellectual maturity, nor physical maturity, nor spiritual maturity, but emotional maturity, and dwelling on popular music could stock the heart with a treasury of finely nuanced feelings and sentiments. Every album I purchased offered the possibility of entrance into some unknown, previously unidentified realm of desire, love, sublimity, or regal woe. Insofar as I wanted to be a human being, popular music taught me how.

When I was twenty-two, in desperate need of cash, I sold every CD I owned save two, the *Lost In Translation* soundtrack and Third Eye

Blind's eponymous album (the faithful remnant), and moved from
Moscow, Idaho to Chicago and lived with a friend there for a year. I
purchased an iPod and used my roommate's computer to load it with
songs—all of which were pirated. In 2005, I moved back to Moscow,
shortly thereafter I began dating Paula (who also moved back), and we
married in 2006. During our first two years of marriage, we were quite
poor and I purchased very little music. I was also largely ignorant of
where and how to steal music on the internet, so I lived off the music
still on my iPod. When that iPod died in 2008, I owned almost no
music; thus I began the tedious and expensive process of rebuilding my
collection.

While I lived in Moscow, all of my music purchases were made at a
store called Hastings, a chain of big box stores which sold books, movies, CDs, video games, and computer software. In addition to selling
new CDs, Hastings also bought and sold used CDs, and every purge
of my CD collection meant carrying several crates into Hastings and
coming out an hour later with a small sum of cash. Hastings sold used
CDs for around half the cost of new CDs, and I could sell used CDs
to Hastings for two or three dollars cash, or four or five dollars in store
credit. Shortly after my iPod died in 2008, the Moscow Hastings began
a pilot program of buying and selling used books, as well. I was then
matriculating at the University of Idaho, and on a few occasions, I traded college books into Hastings for a pittance in credit. The collection of
Grace Paley's short stories for which I paid twenty-four dollars—and,
upon finishing, vowed to never touch again—netted me around eight
dollars in Hastings credit. Obviously, this was a terrible return, but it
was far better than nothing at all.

   During this time, our second year of marriage, my wife and I took a
trip to Los Angeles and spent the week with her uncle. During this trip,
whilst waiting for my wife to try on an armful of clothes in a Banana
Republic, I was standing in an outdoor mall, thinking of nothing at all,

when a wonderful and ill-fated thought flittered through my head: Can I buy used books for cheap and resell them at a higher price? A moment later, my wife emerged from the store and the thought of reselling books did not recur to me again for more than a week.

Back in Moscow, however, one afternoon I recalled the idea and I drove to the Goodwill, where I paid five dollars for two hardback books and two paperbacks. I spent no more than two minutes selecting the titles, but found the newest looking titles I could, and ones in good condition. The Goodwill was less than a mile from Hastings. Ten minutes after paying five dollars for these four books, a sales clerk at Hastings ran the ISBN numbers through their system and said, "We can offer you twenty-seven dollars in credit for these books."

Obviously, I agreed to these terms. However, as soon as the gift card was in my hand, I began wondering whether what I had just done was moral, let alone legal. These uncertainties did not prevent me from immediately using the gift card, though later that afternoon, I lay on the sofa and spent an hour replaying the matter in my head, trying to discern if I had broken the law. No matter how I cut it, though, the whole affair seemed entirely above board. Converting five dollars into twenty-seven dollars in less than twenty minutes struck me as profoundly unfair, though I could not initially say who was being cheated. Did Goodwill not want to sell books? Did Hastings not want to buy books? Did I not want a massive return on a paltry investment? After much consideration, I decided that I was simply quite clever, like John D. Rockefeller, or the fellow who invented sticky notes. Over the next two years, I spent eight hundred dollars acquiring used books. I exchanged those used books for around ten-thousand dollars in credit at Hastings.

I learned to sniff out used books wherever they were hiding. Certain hallways of the University campus were commonly used as dumping grounds for professors who were cleaning their offices. Most libraries have a rack of books they sell for a dollar each. I learned which Goodwill stores stocked the best books, and how Hastings' purchasing software determined buyback prices. Hardback books paid better than paperback, non-fiction paid better than fiction, current bestsellers paid better than anything else. Occasionally, a loophole in the system created an unusually high price for a one-off title. Used hardback copies of *The Celestine Prophesy* are as common as daisies, but between 2008 and 2010, I sold twenty copies of that book to Hastings for around eight dollars each. Current hardback fad diet books showed up at Goodwill every day, all of them one dollar and forty-nine cents, and each one returned ten dollars to twelve dollars at Hastings. Twice a year, at the end of the local Friends of the Library book sale, I filled grocery bags of books for a dollar each, then resold each bag for forty dollars to Hastings. The man purchasing a particular used book for ten dollars is mostly paying for the convenience of someone else finding it for him. However, the man looking for just any old used books need not pay much for them. The world is inundated with unsorted used books which are practically being thrown away. For well over a year, I brought a liquor store box of books into Hastings twice a week and walked away each time with around eighty dollars in credit. Everyone knew my name. No one asked where the books came from.

Within a few months, I had cleared every CD out of the local Hastings store which I was interested in and moved on to the Hastings website, which had lower prices and a more diverse selection. In high school, I was careful, studious, meticulous in every purchase I made. With six hundred dollars in Hastings credit to spend every month, I quit buying albums and started buying whole catalogs. Everything Depeche Mode ever put out. Everything by the Cure. Everything by David Bowie. Everything by U2. Everything by The Jesus & Mary Chain. After six months of combing the website, I had gone from purchasing albums I knew were good to purchasing albums I had heard of. For months, two or three CDs came in the mail every day, and I stayed up until two in the morning scouring the website, looking for more things to buy.

Describing the change such purchasing power had on my state of mind will prove difficult. I lived in a constant state of mild anxiety. From the moment I clicked the purchase button at night to the moment the purchased items arrived a week later, I suffered an agitation and worry akin to that of man who suspects his boss has completely misunderstood something he said. I said to myself, "What if the CDs I ordered do not come? And these were the most important CDs I have yet ordered! The rest of them can be thrown into the ocean, the only ones I really wanted are, right now, tenuously caught in the peril of the postal service!" As soon as the CDs arrived, however, I immediately lost interest in them. I had never really wanted them in the first place. Rather, I had *wanted* to want them. Having acquired them, I could not *want* to want them any longer. I simply had to want them, and I didn't.

Nearly a hundred CDs arrived every month, though I listened to very few of them. As a teenager, I would listen to a new CD front to back, while reclining on my bed, the lyrics in the liner notes open in my lap. Now, I would pop a new CD in from time to time and listen to the first ten seconds of every song. If a song did not immediately arrest my interest, I could not be bothered to give it the benefit of the doubt, hear it to the end, learn to like it. I had so much music to work through, there was not time. It was no longer my responsibility to find music interesting. Rather, it was the responsibility of music to be interesting. Often enough, I did not even listen to the first ten seconds of all the songs, just the first five songs, and if the first ten seconds of the first five songs was not sufficiently compelling, I moved on to the next CD and told myself, "I will bother some other time." With the great surplus of music which came flooding into my home, I quit listening to music I actually enjoyed. All my time was spent testing out new music, which I rarely liked as much as the records I purchased back in high school. Every record for which I know all the lyrics was purchased before I turned eighteen.

When I tell this story to my students, they are quick to refer to my "addiction to buying music." The ancients do not often speak of addiction, though, and neither does Scripture. They speak of slavery and tyranny. To say that I was addicted to buying music makes it sound as though I was powerless, bereft of bargaining rights. In fact, I had become the master of something to which I had formerly submitted myself. When British rock band Oasis released *Be Here Now* on August 26, 1997, I walked three miles to the mall and was present at Sam Goody when the doors opened so that I could be the first person in town to buy it, own it, adore it. I cannot recall for certain, but I believe I wore a coat and tie for the event.

While I am ready to admit my love of music was idolatrous, such idolatry was not without certain ennobling aspects. Many, many years later, when I finally began to study literature and philosophy which was worthy of my time, I had already cultivated a lifelong habit of reading deeply into things. The idea that divine things had many stubborn layers of meaning was intuitive. By the time I moved from Radiohead to Rousseau, I had spent more than a decade practicing submission to the text. I had learned that a text is not a stack of blocks, and the interpretation of the text is not simply a rearrangement of the blocks, none left unused. I had learned from popular music that a text is more like a liver. It works, but you do not know how. You need it, but you do not know why. However, with a monthly music allowance which rivaled payments on a new Mercedes, the problem was not addiction, but blasphemy. A man is far better off serving foreign gods than imagining himself a god. With unbounded access to music, music became common, even banal. If being enslaved to music had been bad, enslaving music to myself was worse.

The conclusion of this story is absurd, though predictable: after two years of the Hastings charade, I moved to Florida, where there were no Hastings stores. Having spent two years expanding and deepening my wants, I was suddenly removed from the ability to satisfy them. My first several months in Florida were disorienting. Bereft of the money or credit to buy new CDs, I began listening to the thousands of CDs I had purchased during the Hastings years. I discovered that most of them were not to my taste and thus began selling them off for a fraction of what it cost to acquire them. To this day, I own perhaps just one hundred of the two thousand CDs that came from Hastings.

The Hastings affair also significantly altered my taste in music. Around the time I moved from the Northwest to the Gulf Coast, where the nearest Hastings was more than two hundred miles away, I heard Tim Hecker's "I'm Transmitting Tonight" and fell down the rabbit hole of ambient music. Having amassed the collection of pop music I had always dreamed of, I no longer really wanted it. I had moved on.

High school students are not situated such that Boethius's cautions against money will easily take hold of their imaginations. Adult warnings about the slipperiness of wealth tend to strike high school students, who have no money, as rather self-serving. After all, adults have all the money in the world, and they often seem far stingier with it than teenagers think fair. From time to time, adults of North America divest themselves of three grand just to get new gutters put on the house, and yet they sigh and choke as though twenty dollars for a movie is going to break the bank. I describe the Hastings affair in such detail because, at seventeen, I was fairly convinced I could live a much fuller life if I had only a fuller collection of music. I lavished my hours on record stores, wallet empty, flipping through titles and curating lists in my head of what I wanted and how much I wanted it. But nearly everyone has a hobby, and nearly everyone is beset by some delusional yearning for a particular cut, style, or variety of earthly good. We make such items idols when we tell ourselves that earthly goods are capable of making us content, for contentment is a state of the spirit, not the body. Further, contentment is a virtue, and to treat an earthly object as though it has the power to confer virtue on its possessor is blasphemous.

Christ alone is possessed unto the virtue of the possessor. I am not suggesting that the desire for any earthly thing is blasphemous, or that the man who eagerly awaits the release of a motion picture is placing his soul in jeopardy. The virtuous soul has many loves, and yet they are rightly ordered such that passing things are not preferred over eternal things. Earthly things are good, in and of themselves, but we are fools if we do not recognize the speed and prowess with which earthly things oust ultimate things from the thrones of our hearts. I can go for days without praying and not really notice it, but I cannot go for days without eating. I have gone weeks without reading the Bible and scarcely noticed it, but my blood itches when I impose a two-day fast from Facebook on myself. Jesus is not everything to me, and I am not certain I have ever met anyone for whom Jesus is everything. From time to time, I feel the sad truth of this statement more acutely, then I pray, confess my sins, and redouble my efforts to serve other people and shun vice, but such resolutions of spirit often do not last the weekend. My other, lesser desires return, and I once again behave as though a gracious surplus of money, liquor, food, or time to myself would make my life better. The ultimate banality of money is a lesson most Americans must learn over and over again.

Another time, years after Hastings, I suddenly came into a windfall of money. With little advance notice, I found a thousand-dollar cash gift in my wallet. At the time, I was not accustomed to having more than fifty dollars in my wallet at any point during the average month. Just after Christmas I might have more, but from day to day, I had little spending money. What is more, this thousand dollars entered my pocket during the first week of summer vacation, and two months lay open before me in which I could spend it. And to make matters better still, my wife and I were on the cusp of a three-week trip to Seattle, where there were far better things to spend money on than there were in the much smaller city I came from. Before I told my wife about the money, I decided I would split it down the middle with her, then went to the bank for a variety of small bills, which I variously distributed among the pockets of my jeans and suit jacket. When I got home, I said to her, "Didn't you say you wanted to get your haircut before our trip?" and I reached in my back pocket and pulled out forty dollars, which I handed to her. She accepted it happily, a little confused, and said, "Where did this come from?" I then said, "And while you're out getting your haircut, why don't you treat yourself to lunch?" and took a twenty dollar bill from a different pocket, then handed it to her. "And after lunch, why don't you go to the mall and find a new dress to wear on the plane?" and I handed her another sixty dollars from the breast pocket of my coat. "And while you're at the mall, you will probably want to get some coffee," and I pulled a five from the lapel pocket. So on and so forth, I continued pulling cash from different pockets and absent-mindedly suggesting she should get other things for herself, and after the third or fourth suggestion, she stood before me, laughing, her hands open and slowly filling with cash until she was holding five hundred dollars.

Several days later, we flew to Seattle.

For the man who is typically broke, a sudden and massive influx of money stands to significantly alter his worldview, for the world suddenly goes from being an unaffordable place to being an affordable place. Unaffordable things do not really exist. However, affordable things are very real, and so with a tidy sum of spendable cash, previously unseen and unknown objects gradually begin to materialize all around a man. It is almost as though poverty is a hazy film which covers the eyes of the poor and money is the antidote which begins to heal the eyes. Had I no money upon arriving in Seattle, I would have spent my time reading, watching films, writing, cooking, talking with my wife, playing with my children. As it was, I spent my time shopping, and when the stores closed, I kept shopping online.

To my credit, I have never really had a taste for costly gadgets. For the man with a hankering for state-of-the-art headphones, five hundred dollars might mean a few hours of research, a single purchase, and a single item received in the mail. Most of the things I wanted (as a child, as an adult) cost less than twenty dollars, which means that five hundred dollars is not merely a lot of money, it is a lot of individual purchases. That summer, I bought books. I bought records. I bought clothes. I bought fancy chocolate I couldn't afford and didn't need. I spent the first week scouring Amazon and Banana Republic for deals, for baubles, for things I could barely remember wanting years ago. After seven days, I had rolled through half my money, at which point I did a sudden about face.

I had planned on this money lasting me the whole summer, and I was on pace to go dry before the 4th of July. When my wallet hit two hundred and fifty dollars, I resolved to slow down, but this proved harder than I would have thought. Having passed the last ten days doing nothing more than spending money (and, when not spending money, thinking about what I could spend money on), when I tried to go back to enjoying life as it came, I found myself disoriented. It might take a man a year to sink into the habit of jogging three miles every morning, but a man quickly acclimatizes to spending money. As opposed to the mild thrill I enjoyed from spending money during my first week, my second week in Seattle likewise unfolded as a sequence of purchases, but each purchase was attended by a sinking sense of guilt and anxiety which had been absent the first week. Not even the retail zing could abate the morose feeling that I was heaping up unhappiness for myself.

By the end of our three week stay, I had emptied my wallet. No money remained. Beside this, I was returning to Florida with roughly fifty additional pounds of goods and there was no room in my luggage for any of it, which meant all my books, tapes, clothes, garbage, and mammon had to be mailed three thousand miles. The cost to mail a wasted vacation home was a hundred and twenty dollars, paid with credit and buyer's remorse.

When I got back to Florida, I waited for the box, but it never came. Two days passed, three days, four days. When I finally had the presence of mind to track the package, I found that it had come within twenty yards of my front door, but an illegible address had rendered it undeliverable. The package was returned to the sender, the address all the way back in Seattle. In the day which following my learning this, disbelief gave way to anger, anger gave way to disappointment. Finally, I confessed to my wife, "I deserved this," and gave up hope of ever seeing it again.

Weeks later, miraculously, the box returned to me, though I was nearly as disappointed at the arrival of the box as I was at its disappearance earlier. Had everything gained during those three weeks turned out a complete and unequivocal loss, the lesson would have been seared more deeply, more permanently into my conscience. As I unpacked my box, however, I could feel myself become a bit more foolish with every recovered object I placed on a shelf, in a drawer, or hung in a closet. The ultimate restoration of my lost goods was no more a gift of God than is a hangover after a night of hard, distempered drinking. Getting my things back was a hard providence.

This all transpired seven years ago, and today, with the exception of a single CD, everything in that box was slowly lost, broken, sold, given away, or thrown away. Unironically, the lone surviving object is a CD entitled Sour Times.

The best part of having that thousand dollars was giving the first half to my wife, and I claim this not as a sentimentalist, but a sybarite. In terms of real enjoyment, real thrill, and real return on dollars spent, slowly surprising my wife with five hundred dollars in small bills was more raw, uncut fun than anything else I did with the money. Even if I were not a Christian, put no stock in charity or generosity, and had nothing to anticipate after death, honesty would nonetheless compel me to confess none of the money was so enjoyable to part with as that which returned to earthly good or service.

None of this should be taken to mean I no longer yearn for earthly things. In the last seven years, I have hankered and ached for a record, a book, a jacket, a pair of shoes, a bottle of liquor which was fifty dollars more than I could ever justify spending. However, when I have the presence of mind to consider such hankerings within the broader context of my life, I can confront present lusts with the bracing fact that none of my desires lasts that long. What I ought to do with my wants is wait them out.

When I tell such stories to my students, I do not expect them to suddenly give up their own wants simply "because an adult told me they would not pan out." Boethius is not under the delusion that his readers will live carefree, simple lives just because he instructed them to do so in his little book. However, Boethius is providing readers with a rubric for interpreting their own loss, their own disappointment. As a philosopher writing a philosophical text, he assumes his readers have seen the value in examining, pondering, and interpreting their own lives. Students of fifteen or sixteen are not too young to begin reflecting on their own responses to loss, or to note the tragicomic wax and wane of their desire

> **"The more varied your precious possessions, the more help you need to protect them, and the old saying is proved correct, he who hath much, wants much."**
> **-Lady Philosophy, 2.5 (p. 35)**

L onging leads to having, and having leads to longing. He who has much, wants much. The proverb proves true not only for money, but possessions, power, pleasure. He who has much power also wants much power. He who has much sex also wants much sex. He who has much liquor also wants much liquor. No man is rich in life who shakes and groans, desperate to live longer; the more desperately a man clings to life, the less he has to live for. The more zealously an older woman clings to youth, the more grotesque she becomes.

Of all the difficult ideas in *The Consolation*, the chapters on having and lacking will likely prove the hardest for the American teenager to believe. "Money cannot buy you happiness" sounds like the kind of pious but vacuous cant which middle class adults are obligated to parrot for their children. Pious, for it sounds like something Christ would say in the Sermon on the Mount, but vacuous, for what child has not heard his parents unhappily sigh, "We just don't have the money for it. Perhaps another time." Besides, every teenager has been forced to turn down a friend's invitation to the movies or the beach simply because he does not have the money for it, and he hears later his friend had a fine time and he, too, might have had a fine time had he just a bit more cash. Very few people need a lot more money. "No man is rich who shakes and groans, convinced that he needs more," says Lady Philosophy, but not a lot more. Just more. Let us be reasonable: a little more. But a little more money is the most aggravating sum of money a man can need. If someone ever writes a book called *A Natural History of Temptation*, the first chapter should be entitled "Just the Tiniest Bit More."

In Book IV of *Paradise Lost*, Milton's Satan ruminates on why he rebelled and concludes that the great glory God first endowed him with was the chief reason. Satan perceives just how narrow the expanse is which separates his own majesty from the Divine majesty. To dwell so close to the top, and yet not, is grating. For the angel who lives in the mediocre middle, possessing but lukewarm majesty, the expanse separating himself from the top is intimidatingly vast. In the temptation of Eve, Satan impresses his own image upon the unsuspecting woman. Has God really made you lords of the Earth? No. He has made you lords of nearly the whole Earth. One lonely tree separates you from unqualified dominion.

An old proverb, claimed by nearly every nation on the earth, is instructive when explaining these chapters of *The Consolation* to my students:

One drink is just right,
Two is too many,
Three is too few.

Two is too many because, in reaching for the second drink, a man has succumbed to a dangerous logic. If one drink can provide pleasure, so can two, but so can three. The key leap in the proverb is not between the second and third lines, but the first and the third. The man who has only one drink is "just right" because his desire was not for pleasure, but for a drink. Having had his drink, he does not need another. The man who has two drinks, however, does not really want a drink, but the pleasure which comes from a drink. Given that he wants pleasure, not drinks, no amount of drinks will ever satisfy him.

Consider two different people at an all-you-can-eat buffet: an obese man and a little child. The little child fills a plate of food, then has a dish of ice cream, then says he is finished. The obese man fills one plate of food, then another, then another, then another. When he is hungry, he eats, and when he eats, food tastes good. However, when he is no longer hungry, food still tastes good. Roast beef does not begin to taste like rotten eggs simply because a man has had enough.

The man who continues to eat after he is no longer hungry does not want to be satisfied; rather, he wants pleasure. Satisfaction is the cessation of want, the ending of desire. In a sense, satisfaction is also the cessation of pleasure. The act of satisfying our wants gives pleasure, but after the point of satisfaction is reached, the thing which gave us pleasure remains pleasurable. The obese man may keep eating even after he is full, but in so doing, he is also expanding his desires, for desires are elastic. If we starve them, they will shrink, and if we stuff them, they will grow. He who has much, wants much. The obese man has rejected satisfaction in favor of pleasure; he does not want to be satisfied by food. Satisfaction or contentment is enjoyed in the soul, not the body, but pleasure is experienced in the body, so in order to keep eating, the glutton must silence his soul. His soul is trying to tell his body to stop. "I am satisfied," says the soul, after a plate or two of food. "I do not care," replies the body. The body may continue to experience pleasure at the expense of the soul; the soul is a kind of fuel source from which the body may draw. If the body is willing to burn a bit of the soul, a little more pleasure can be gained. A man who refuses to wait for his wife can look at pornography, which is to say he can break off a chunk of his soul, sacrifice it to Dionysus, and Dionysus will repay the man so much pleasure in return. A man may sacrifice the interests of his body to Christ, who will repay with virtue, or a man may sacrifice the interests of his soul to Dionysus, who will repay with the pleasures of vice.

Silencing the soul that the body may enjoy pleasure is dangerous and disorienting, though. The glutton at the buffet will eventually leave the restaurant because he becomes bored or has something else to do. He may comment to a friend that the food was delicious, but the deliciousness means very little to him. The food has been reduced to mere material, for it has no intellectual or spiritual significance. While the obese man has obtained more pleasure than the little boy who ate a single plate and a dish of ice cream, he has no satisfaction. In order to eat so much, he must bind and gag his soul. The obese man who eats seven plates of food is no more sated than a large doll which has seven plates of food crammed down its plastic throat. The doll has no soul, and through the sinful indulgence of appetite, the obese man has silenced his soul.

The interests of the body and the interests of the soul are like two wrestlers within a man, each attempting to subdue the other. Every man may feed, train, and strengthen these wrestlers however he chooses. When he reads and meditates on Scripture, prays, fasts, goes to church, gives to the poor, or performs works of mercy in secret, he strengthens the spiritual wrestler. When he eats too much, wastes his time on sensual amusements, indulges in sexual perversion, spends his money like a prodigal or shirks his duties, he strengthens the physical wrestler. In moments of temptation, the spiritual wrestler and physical wrestler do battle with one another; if the man spends his days lavishing the physical wrestler with care, he will quickly cave when Satan invites the man to steal pleasure for his body.

The analogy of the two wrestlers is ancient, although modern students uniquely benefit from the appeal to sport. Every kind of sport involves both practice and competition, and everyone who has played a sport knows that practice often involves performing drills which are, in and of themselves, meaningless in a game. A basketball team will run suicides during practice, but if the team began running suicides during a live competition, they would lose before halftime.

While suicides will not win a basketball game, a basketball game cannot be won without suicides. Running suicides teaches endurance when very little is on the line, but that same ability to endure can be taken into a game when much is on the line. The strength gained by lifting weights in a gymnasium is not confined to the gym, but is taken by the gymnast out into the world. So, too, a man gains self-control by fasting, even though the pleasure of food is no vice. The self-control acquired in fasting is not confined to the table or the kitchen, but is carried out into the world where a man is better equipped to decline wicked pleasures. If a man wants to turn down vicious pleasures in the moment of temptation, he must practice turning down allowable pleasures.

A great many products in a capitalist society are perfectly calibrated to be enjoyable, pleasurable, but not satisfactory. A man eats potato chips because the chips are delicious, but he eats the whole bag because they are not satisfying. If the chips were satisfying, he could eat a handful and be done. If a television show is any good, a man will not want to watch eight episodes in a single evening. A single episode of *The Crown* is sufficiently weighty that a second episode is not needed during a single evening. On the other hand, in our early days of marriage, my wife and I would watch three or four episodes of Lost in a row, and only fatigue sent us to bed. Episodes of *The Office* are similarly crunchy, salty, but light and especially unsatisfying in small quantities. One year for Lent, I resolved to only listen to music that was more than a hundred years old. I listened to very little music for forty days, because Beethoven's *Ninth* symphony did not rile up desires for more music, but satisfied my desire for music altogether. Having finished the *Ninth*, listening to more music seemed gratuitous, gluttonous, absurd, like waking in the morning only to take a nap. On the other hand, when I am finished listening to

Depeche Mode's *Black Celebration*, I generally put *Music For The Masses* on. Most popular culture is vaporous enough to disappear from a man's soul in just a few hours. Very few of the movies I watch linger in my imagination longer than the afternoon. Generally speaking, popular culture is not demanding, and so it does not repay repeated viewings or repeated listenings. Depeche Mode requires little, and offers just as little in return.

> **"Let men compose themselves and live at peace,**
> **Set haughty fate beneath their feet,**
> **And look unmoved on fortune good and bad,**
> **And keep unchanging countenance ... "**
> **-Lady Philosophy, 1.4 (p. 8)**

In our day, the word "stoic" usually suggests a man capable of burying his emotions beneath a changeless face. The stoic maintains a stony façade against misfortune, unmoved in the midst of a storm. Such usage of the word is not unfair, however, in Boethius's day, Stoicism was a complete and formidable philosophy. Lady Philosophy makes regular references to Stoic philosophy, and never to condemn it, although Christians of late antiquity were not of one mind about Stoic philosophy. Stoics were pagan philosophers who recognized that the god is good and without change, and that man must conform his life to a good, unchanging god. Further, Stoics held that god is omnipresent, at all times and in all places filling all things, and that god does not change according to his circumstances, for he is not susceptible to material influence. For Stoics, god is virtue itself, god is always perfectly satisfied, god is wholly self-sustaining, god is spirit. The satisfaction of god depends entirely on his virtue. So, too, a godly man will not change according to his circumstances, be they good or bad. He looks "unmoved on fortune good and bad," as the Lady says.

Stoics identified four ways in which a man was given to change based on his fortune: desire, delight, fear, and grief, all of which Lady Philosophy references in her poetry. Like god, Stoics believed a man ought to be content in virtue alone. Our contentment should not rest on whether we get the pay raise we desire, or whether the cancer screening comes back negative. If a man stakes the tranquility of his soul on physical things, his life will be unstable, for the material world is constantly changing.

Modern Christians will have a hard time accepting Stoic philosophy. Even in Boethius's day, the extent to which Christians could accept Stoic philosophy was contested. In the *City of God*, Augustine vouches for the four Stoic passions. We ought to fear displeasing God, he claims. We ought to grieve when we displease God. This might strike us as a paltry defense of a dynamic life, for in Ecclesiastes 3, Solomon prescribes a time not merely for the passions, but a time for all things, including hate, mourning, weeping, laughing, and dancing.

Jesus wept, as did St. Peter, and it was right they wept, despite what Stoics say.

While I am not entirely comfortable with Boethius's forthright endorsement of Stoic philosophy, there is far more to gain than lose from his Stoic predilections. Lady Philosophy sees the wild fluctuations of anger and sadness which have overtaken Boethius and she suggests he ought to have expected poor treatment at the hands of Fortune. He should have been making room in his soul for such injustice so that when it came, his heart would not be overthrown. A man can become immune to death by acclimatizing to it over the course of his life; however, Boethius has failed to do this. Because Boethius has not forced little misfortunes on himself in small acts of self-denial, when misfortune attacks him from without, he is unprepared. "It is hardly surprising," says the Lady, "if we are driven by the blasts of storms when our chief aim on this sea of life is to displease wicked men," subtly implying that Boethius's chief aim in life was something else, given his shock at how poorly his life is turning out.

It was not until my third or fourth reading of *The Consolation* that I truly understood the value of living in such a way that great change was not necessary. We may balk at the idea of becoming rigorous Stoics, but neither will the prudent man run the opposite direction from Stoicism. Most men use promises of great change in the future to justify their present vices and immaturity. My students regularly tell me that they rarely read their Bibles and do not often pray, but that they have sworn to themselves they will do both pious tasks with great zeal once they move away for college. Teenage boys lie to their mothers to get what they want, but tell themselves they would never lie to their wives. College students promise themselves they will not drink so much in the future, or that they will not need pornography once they are married. Married women swear they will read the Bible more to their children than they read it for themselves. Even if they cannot tend to their own souls properly, they will properly tend to the souls of their children. In brief, many people behave as though the stage of life they are currently in is the hardest, most complex and demanding stage of life there is; the contradictions and demands of the present stage make it difficult to pursue virtue now. However, the next stage in life will be far simpler, more peaceful, and pursuing virtue will become easier once the next stage has been attained. Autonomy will make it easy to be good. A girlfriend will make virtue attainable. Money will make virtue attainable. Children, a career, a house with a little more room will bring righteousness near to me.

But I laugh. I say, "You will not read your Bible more in the future. You will simply be very good at not reading your Bible." If a man spends the first two decades of his life refining a certain skill, he will not summarily give up that ability overnight. The boy who develops the power to deceive his mother in order to get what he wants will have no ability to be honest with his wife. The man who quickly consoles himself with liquor in college will only find additional anxieties attend the life of a husband and father. The young woman who devotes every leisure hour to her own amusement and luxury will not suddenly find delight in a demanding child. Virtue requires practice. The complacent man is not being transfigured from a lesser kind of creature to something greater, he is becoming more deeply entrenched in his current habit of being. If a high school sophomore wants to read his Bible as an adult, he must read his Bible as a teenager. If a young woman does not want her soul to be vexed and overthrown by the all-consuming needs of an infant, she should begin making room for that infant as early as she can. "Sufficient for the day is its own trouble," teaches Christ, and He makes this claim generically, universally. Christ does not say this is true for the poor only, or minorities only, or widows only, or adults only. Life is harder for some people than others, though life is sufficiently difficult for everyone. Even little children have their work cut out. In Ecclesiastes, Solomon teaches his son to "Remember your Creator in the days of your youth, before the days of trouble come and the years approach when you will say, I find no pleasure in them," as though life becomes increasingly difficult, and piety in youth is necessary to fight the bitterness which otherwise sets in with old age.

The virtuous life does not require regular upheavals of spirit, but anticipates future suffering and begins preparing for the many epochs of varied responsibility which lie ahead. A man's life passes in a series of stages: infancy, childhood, adolescence, then the sudden burst of freedom which comes with college. After college, engagement, marriage, the first child, the second child. Finally, sons and daughters begin leaving home, the empty nest, retirement, old age, then the time of many funerals, and finally death. Each of these stages of life comes with particular temptations, trials, labors, expectations, privileges, rights, and cultural expectations. The world makes allowances for every age, so when a two-year old pitches a screaming fit, any reasonable onlooker will think, "My two-year-old did the same. It is only to be expected." When a junior boy is caught smoking a joint in the parking lot after a basketball game, his parents might be angry, but they ought not be shocked and outraged. We do not make allowances for sin, but we allow that certain temptations weigh more heavily on us at particular stages of life. On the other hand, if the gym teacher is caught smoking a joint in the parking lot after a game, outrage is an entirely appropriate response. Maturity entails accepting the responsibilities which attend any stage of life, but rejecting the allowances society makes for certain sins typical of that stage. The mature man understands that the responsibilities of one stage often carry over to the next stage, but the allowances typically do not. Lingering on every allowance made for every stage of life ultimately leads to immaturity and regular bloody revolutions of the will.

For example, take that stage of life in which a child is on the cusp of entering adolescence. Invariably, there comes that moment when a child's friends begin leaving toys behind. A boy goes to the home of his friend to play, brings a two-foot plastic pirate sword, and, upon arriving, his friend produces a small pocket knife and says, "I don't want to play with fake swords. I want a real one." Or a girl brings a princess doll to her friend's home, but her friend shows her a stick of lip gloss, applies some to her own lips, and says, "I don't want to pretend my doll is fancy. I want to be the doll. I want to be fancy." She has tired of using an avatar. She wants to become the thing which she has formerly used to explore the world. Every movement from one stage of life to the next requires existential sacrifice. The ten-year-old boy does not move from a two-foot pirate sword to a two-foot real sword. Rather, he trades a two-foot pirate sword for a two-inch Swiss Army knife. The little girl does not trade a doll's gown for a real gown, rather, she trades a plastic princess for a bit of blush. The gauntlet which separates one stage from the next is simply a person's willingness to go from top-seeded amateur to bottom-ranked pro. A human being is so desperate for the real, for the transcendent, that he is willing to trade a spectacular illusion for a paltry truth. Only truth can so compel a man upwards. The highest allowances of a dating relationship are traded for the awkwardness of marriage. The closest intimacy allowed husband and wife are exchanged for the glorious estrangements which come with a first child. A man reaches the apex of his career and then enters the disorientation of retirement, an escape from servile labor unto pure aristocratic leisure. Entry into the next stage does not come without something feigned, something performed. When a young boy sees his friend has begun to play with a pocket knife, he does not immediately lose interest in his plastic pirate sword. Rather, he is caught between two realities, one lower and one higher. Desire for the higher reality is performed, and desire for the lower reality is artificially and painfully hidden, scuttled. When the boy tells his father, "My friend has a pocket knife and I was wondering if I could have one, too," his father gives him no definite answer, but says, "Well, let's see if you can handle the responsibility which comes with a knife. Mow the lawn every Saturday for the next two months, and do so without my reminding you, and I will know you are ready for a knife." His father requires the desire for the privilege of the next stage be matched with the responsibility, and in assuming the responsibility, whether the boy enjoys mowing the lawn or not, proves not that the boy is ready for the next stage, but that the boy is already there. His father requires his son to seize the maturity appropriate to the knife, and so the boy does not so much earn the knife as he rises, like a flame, to the place where owning a knife is only natural. The boy enters a higher reality and the world follows him. Of course, this is not merely true of adolescence, but every stage in human life. Maturity is the pantomime of maturity. The changeless, Stoic face which Lady Philosophy commends against misfortune is the maturity of a living man looking forward to death. After junior high comes high school. After high school comes college. After college comes marriage. And yet every stage of life looks forward to death, the bodiless era of man's existence in which he must negotiate reality without any material indulgence. If the junior high student must assume high school responsibilities in order to be worthy of high school allowances, the living man must assume deathly responsibilities in order to be worthy of deathly privileges. Death is a practical problem, but life provides more than ample time to sort out death.

The wise man knows what stage of life he is currently in, but keeps his eye on the next two stages of life. The dating man goes to the engaged man and says, "What does the Devil try next?" The engaged man goes to the married man and says, "What does the Devil try next?" A wise man will begin making room in his spirit for both the pains and the temptations of the next stage. Movement from one stage to the next happens both by nature and by human striving. In the early stages of life, a man naturally becomes stronger and more dexterous; greater ability means greater responsibility. If a young man believes that he will inevitably become an adult, he is right, in a certain sense. There is a kind of intellectual and spiritual maturity which tends to go along with physical maturity, but the former does not naturally outpace the latter. Maturity takes place when the responsibilities of the next stage are undertaken before they *must be* undertaken, and the allowances of the present stage are abandoned. The mature man willingly takes on new labors and willingly lets go of old rights; time will ultimately force him to do both, but the wise man knows he responds poorly to compulsion. What this means is that a young man or woman, let us say, recognizes that in American culture, a certain lenience is granted to teenage foolishness: a love of silly music and comic books, giggling, gossip, petty flirtation, chapped lips, slovenly appearance, crass jokes, mindless chatter and so forth. If an adult embodied all these predictably teenage idiosyncrasies, that person might be thought mad, but much leeway is granted for teenagers in these things. Upon realizing that his foolishness is merely being given leeway, a prudent teenager sees that the right to terrible music and wrinkled clothes must be renounced in order to move into the coming stages of life. He also comprehends that the longer he exercises these rights, the more painful it will be to give them up, and the more likely he will be to never completely leaving them behind. Every teenager has known grown men who have failed to become actual adults, and while he might joke that there is something awesome about a married man with kids who still has a poster of Scarlett Johansson in her *Avengers* latex catsuit framed in his office, he is also secretly unsettled by this. The oldest woman in the club is an embarrassment, but she is also the woman who was the second-oldest in the club last month, the third-oldest last winter, the fourth-oldest last year . . . and the three-hundred-twenty-ninth oldest on the eve of her 21st birthday, when she went out dancing for the first time. She had the cultural right to go out on her twenty-first birthday, but with every passing day, the ultimate unreliability of this right should be increasingly clear to her. The best way to not become the oldest woman in the club is to quit going to the club the moment you realize such a future is distasteful.

After coming to terms with how painful it will be to have rights to pleasure stripped from his clenched fists, the prudent man begins giving up those rights early. The engaged man asks the married man what the Devil does next, the married man replies, "He tempts you to bitterness over how little time you have to yourself," and so the engaged man promptly begins giving up his free time. When maturity comes to collect the man's rights, the man has long practiced letting them go, or else has no free time to give up, and so marriage does not entail great cataclysm. The prudent man lives a sustainable life, not a life wherein forthcoming difficulties are anticipated with disgust.

Such a description of maturity is not exactly the Stoic life, but neither is it wholly opposed to the Stoic life. The Stoic identification of the similarities between virtue and changelessness are apt, sage, lucid. At the same time readers of *The Consolation* should not uncritically accept all Stoic prejudices; an honest man reflecting on the state of his body and soul invariably wishes that he had begun making certain changes long ago. No man wants to confess his use of pornography to his wife, but he does wish that he had confessed it to her a year ago and that the confession was nothing more than an unpleasant, but salvific memory today. No woman wants to tell her husband she has, for years, been in the habit of secretly spending far more money than she lets on; no one wants the hassle of dealing with sin today, but wishes his sin had been dealt with long ago. Such wishes aim toward an unchanging life, a simple life, a divine and Stoic life.

Every pursuit of maturity—made during any stage of life, whether made by a high school sophomore or a man in his retirement—is ultimately preparation for death. If a man is not preparing for death, there is no sense preparing for anything else.

Early in *The Consolation*, we learn Boethius has been sentenced to die for conspiring to overthrow the state, a crime he did not commit. Unlike Job, Boethius gazes back longingly at his former life. In the midst of his suffering, Job does not mention the children he has lost, neither the fortune nor the power he formerly enjoyed. Job does not sin with his mouth because he centers his complaint on the loss of God's favor, not the loss of his things. Job never mentions his children or his wealth to God. He does not grasp at the material blessings which have been torn from his hands. Rather, he wants to see God and hear God's account of Himself. Boethius is outraged at the injustice he has suffered for doing good, like Job, but he is also miserable at having lost his comfortable and prestigious old life. Job cannot be tempted by remembrances of his money, and so when his friends tell him that he should confess his sin and God will restore his wealth, Job is disinterested. On the other hand, much of *The Consolation* involves Lady Philosophy talking Boethius through the loss of his mammon and good luck.

While every Christian benefits in reading of Job's righteous release of the world, every Christian can also gain from reading of Boethius's grasping for the world. The Lady will offer a divine perspective on the loss of power, home, family, wealth, reputation, and if young readers of *The Consolation* have not yet suffered such losses, such losses are nonetheless in the cards.

The loss of his fortune has led Boethius to tire of life. Why, he wonders, does Death let miserable men live and yet take those who are happy? He has some time left before his execution, but bereft of his home, family, honor, wealth, and reputation, he is no longer interested in life.

Job also eggs God on for a face to face meeting, although Job is more interested in justice. Job is not bored with life, but fascinated by the possibilities of life after death. In the early chapters of *The Consolation*, however, we do not hear Boethius longing for the life to come, but bemoaning his bad luck. Boethius has ceased preparing for death, and so life is not worth living.

If home, family, and honor were all that made his life worth living, Boethius's life was inevitably headed toward meaninglessness, whether he was falsely convicted of a capital crime or not. In death, all these things will be taken away. Given that hospitals, hospices, and retirement homes safely hide the dying from the eyes of the young and robust, most Americans think of death as a purely existential problem. We also tend to speak far more confidently and dogmatically about what happens to the soul of a man upon death than Scripture or Christian tradition really gives warrant. In 2 Corinthians 5, we read St. Paul teach:

> *So we are always confident, knowing that while we are at home in the body we are absent from the Lord. For we walk by faith, not by sight. We are confident, yes, well pleased rather to be absent from the body and to be present with the Lord. Therefore we make it our aim, whether present or absent, to be well pleasing to Him. For we must all appear before the judgment seat of Christ, that each one may receive the things done in the body, according to what he has done, whether good or bad. Knowing, therefore, the terror of the Lord, we persuade men; but we are well known to God, and I also trust are well known in our consciences.*

After crafting "present" and "absent" as euphemisms for "dead" and "alive," St. Paul says that Christians make it "our aim, whether dead or alive, to be well pleasing" to God. He does not speak as though the struggle to please God in life is made automatic in death. We should not conduct our lives as though death zeroes out every man's account before the Lord; the reason why we make it our aim to please the Lord is because "we must all appear before the judgment seat of Christ," that we may be repaid for all the things done "in the body, whether good or bad." The average American does not speak of the recently departed in reference to repayment for "good and bad." The typical funeral is rarely a sober affair. I write this all not as someone who is confident that Dante's Mount Purgatory lays ahead, but as one who has been instructed to live as though the good things I do will be of some value to me when I die, and that my vices will not.

CHAPTER THREE

Fortune, Luck, and Salvation

"... you are wasting away in pining and longing for your former good fortune...It is the loss of this which, as your imagination works upon you, has so corrupted your mind... But you are wrong if you think Fortune has changed towards you. Change is her normal behavior, her true nature."

- Lady Philosophy, 2.1 (p. 22-23)

Fortune is a central concept to *The Consolation of Philosophy*; however, my students have always balked when, on the first day we discuss the book, I ask if any of them believe in luck. Their objections are pious enough. "Christians cannot believe in luck," they say, "because Christians believe God is in control of all things." Even my Arminian students become Calvinists when the subject of luck arises. Early on in our study of Boethius, I must bring them to the point where they will not scoff at every reference to "fortune," for the word appears in nearly every chapter.

Several editions of *The Consolation* feature a painting by Coëtivy Master of Fortune's wheel, called *Miniatures from Boethius, Consolation de philosophie* (1460-1470). In it, a woman stands before a large wheel upon which four men are fixed, and the woman's hands gently lay on the rim. The figure sitting on top of the wheel wears a crown and is dressed like a king. The man at three o'clock is falling over, perhaps a little bruised. The man on the bottom wears filthy clothes and hangs on for dear life. The man at nine o'clock is dressed like a merchant or an aristocrat, though not as well as the king.

In fact, the four men are one. Lady Fortune spins her wheel, which is the Earth itself, and as the Earth spins, the fortunes of a man rise and fall. In some variations of the image, each man is draped with a banner or fixed with a placard which, moving clockwise, read: I rule, I have ruled, I have no kingdom, and I will rule again.

Assuming for a moment that the teacher of *The Consolation* has a class of rigidly-Calvinistic students, fortune may nonetheless be accounted for as the mere recognition that no man knows what the future holds. God alone knows the future. Fortune is an icon of man's ignorance of what exactly God is doing. In Ecclesiastes 7, we read, "In the day of prosperity be joyful, But in the day of adversity consider: Surely God has appointed the one as well as the other, so that man can find out nothing that will come after him." Fortune illustrates the Solomonic notion that there are "days of prosperity" and "days of adversity," and that no man knows how long either "day" will last. Days of adversity suddenly intrude upon the life of Job, apropos of nothing, and then great days of prosperity return to Job toward the end of his life. He could have predicted neither.

Fortune is best understood from a phenomenological perspective, not a metaphysical one.

The Old Testament is densely populated with references to both "fortune" and "misfortune," meaning both foreseeable and unforeseeable pleasant events and unpleasant events. In Ecclesiastes 9:11, Solomon is comfortable speaking of the secrecy of God's plans from a common-sense standpoint:

The race is not to the swift,
Nor the battle to the strong,
Nor bread to the wise,
Nor riches to men of understanding,
Nor favor to men of skill;
But time and chance happen to them all.

No matter how swift an Olympic athlete runs, he may trip and fall inches from the finish line and look up only to see the slower man win. No matter how strong the navy is, a storm at sea might sink the fleet. No matter how wise a man is, he might still go broke. And when the slow win the race, and the weak win the war, and the idiot gets rich, we have seen time and chance happen to them all . . . or rather, we have seen Fortune at work, as Lady Philosophy says.

Students understand Fortune in their bones, though. They have all prepared diligently for tests which they have nonetheless failed. They have obeyed their parents all week and been arbitrarily told, on Friday night, that they may not go out with their friends. They have known good little boys who obeyed their parents and died young anyway. They have seen perverts and letches get kind, pretty girlfriends. They have seen that a man can do what a mountain may not: rise up in rebellion against the goodness of God. Even people who claim they do not believe in luck rely on the logic of Fortune's wheel in determining fairness. When a child is spending too long at the water fountain, the teacher scolds with, "You need to give the other children a turn," and the "turn" she references is "a turn of Fortune's wheel." When Fortune does not turn her wheel quickly enough, we sometimes force her hand. There is no principle more precious to the administration of justice among children than "the turn."

But the Lady's task is not to rescue Boethius from jail, or to stall his execution, and neither has she come to cheer him up. She has no interest in reversing his bad turn of Fortune's wheel. She comes to accuse, to reason, to rehabilitate, and to persuade Boethius to a more virtuous life. If she accomplishes her task, Boethius will come to understand how he ought to live around the same time he is led away to die. The Lady is not intimidated by how late such a denouement should come in his life. Her stoic conviction that a changeless life is a good life prompts her belief that every day ought to be lived as the last. There might be no greater tragic irony than the man who lives his last day as though years remain.

Ours is a curious society, though, given what kind of images and dialogue typically attend discussions of "living each day as your last." We think a man is "living each day as his last" if he climbs mountains, tells off his boss, or puts his life in great danger for a thrill. Yet I am haunted by the response a dear friend once gave to the question, "How would you like to die?" He said, "I would like to die slowly and painfully for many months so I have time to repent." Because teachers and students alike quickly lose sight of the point of a classical education, every year I ask my students, "If you knew you were going to die in a car crash on the night you graduated from high school, would going to school still be worth it?" In other words, is a diploma merely the means to an end, or is there some value in studying Boethius beyond the grades which become transcripts, which become scholarships, which become better paying jobs someday? The point of teaching *The Consolation* is not to merely acquaint students with a certain set of arguments, definitions, and contours of thought. *The Consolation* must be taught in the same spirit with which it was written.

In 2013, *The New Yorker* ran an article entitled "Last Call" about a Buddhist monk named Ittetsu Nemoto who helps suicidal Japanese men and women think very carefully through the matter of their own deaths. His purpose is helping people live satisfying lives that they would not want to end. He asks his patients to imagine "…they've been given a diagnosis of cancer and have three months to live. He instructs them to write down what they want to do in those three months. Then he tells them to imagine they have one month left; then a week; then ten minutes. Most people start crying in the course of this exercise, Nemoto among them." The exercise bears a striking resemblance to numerous Christian monastic practices, as well as Christ's parables which end with allusions to the unknowability of one's day of death. Since reading of Nemoto, I have often walked students through a similar series of questions, whittling my way slowly from seven years to a mere sixty seconds. Many students report that with seven years left to live, they might still try to marry and begin a career. The sooner the prospect of death, the more "essential tasks" seem inessential. With a week left to live, most students would still eat and sleep. The man with a mere twenty-four hours left may have ceremonial reasons to eat a meal, but no practical reason to do so. When contemplating what they would do with the final sixty seconds of their lives, every student claims they would pray or sing a hymn to God. When I ask them why they would do these things, they reply these are the only tasks left which have any meaning. I ask, "What would you think of a man who spent his last three minutes alive running for the refrigerator and cramming food into his mouth?" They laugh, but after further reflection they say anyone who would do such a thing must be mad. Of course, no man knows how long he will live, and so the Christian religion commends a life of daily prayer, daily hymns, daily contemplation of God's holiness. When Lady Philosophy tells Boethius, "On the last day of one's life there is a kind of death for Fortune even when she stays with one" (p. 28), she means the man who lives every day as though it is his last has escaped the tyranny of Fortune, and is dead to the world, as St. Paul says in Galatians 6:14)

Students who tell me that they would quit school if they only had two years left to live often say they would spend what time they had left on standard bucket list fare, like travelling to Europe, going to concerts, or merely spending time with friends. Such claims also reveal the reasons why the student is trying to get a diploma in the first place, for a diploma will lead to college, a job, and the money needed to travel or skydive or spend leisure time with friends. "What would you do if you only had a year left to live?" is not a fundamentally different question than "What would you do if you only had fifty years left to live?" Those fifty years include a lot of undesirable responsibilities and necessary evils which an imminent death could conveniently set aside. An imminent death does little in changing the rules a man lives by. Rather, an imminent death makes the point of life embarrassingly clear. It is the wager of a classical education (which is exactly what Lady Philosophy is offering Boethius) that all the study and exams and memorization would be time well spent even if the student died on his way to the stage to collect his diploma. Virtue is valuable for its own sake, not for the sake of some commodity it confers later in life.

"When nature brought you forth from your mother's womb I received you naked and devoid of everything and fed you from my own resources. I was inclined to favour you, and I brought you up—and this is what makes you lose patience with me—with a measure of indulgence, surrounding you with all the splendor and affluence at my command. Now I have decided to withdraw my hand. You have been receiving a favour as one who has had the use of another's possessions, and you have no right to complain as if what you have lost was fully your own. . . . I can say with confidence that if the things whose loss you are bemoaning were really yours, you could never have lost them."

- Lady Philosophy speaks on behalf of Fortune, 2.2 (p. 25)

W hen Lady Philosophy adopts the persona of Fortune, she directly addresses Boethius's frustration over his lost luck. She reminds him that he entered the world with nothing and that he may take nothing but his own soul when he departs this world. "How have I been unfair?" she asks. "What have I taken from you which I did not give you in the first place?" Boethius now regrets placing his happiness and contentment on the pleasant effects of fortune, for once the pleasant effects are removed, he is nonetheless still enslaved to a fickle master. In buying a lottery ticket, a man does not merely risk the cost of the ticket against a small chance of winning. Win or lose, the purchase of a lottery ticket nonetheless subscribes a man to a certain kind of logic, a certain habit of being, namely, the belief that a sudden windfall of unearned money is a desirable thing. However, Lady Philosophy is unconcerned with whether a man wins or loses the lottery. The very act of buying the ticket enlists a man in an ultimately tragic life.

But talk of the lottery can prove too much when teaching *The Consolation*. When Lady Philosophy speaks of fortune, she is not only speaking of things like the lottery or a flower pot falling from an apartment window and cracking an unsuspecting pedestrian's skull. Fortune governs all forms of material success and material success tends to work in predictable ways.

The race is usually to the swift, after all. The battle is often to the strong. Bread is normally to the wise. A dour man may work to make himself likeable by smiling more, greeting his coworkers, bringing them gifts on their birthdays, and find that having made such changes, he is invited out to drinks after work more often than when he grimaced and grunted at everyone. Or an obese woman may become profoundly unhappy with her appearance and so begin a diet and exercise program which slowly helps her regain the form and vitality of her youth. Happier with herself, she smiles more, attracts the interest of men, and is asked out on a date for the first time in several years. Neither of these scenarios strike us as "lucky," for the happy results were planned on and labored over. Nonetheless, they fall under the broad umbrella of Fortune, for the province of Fortune is any and every material condition or situation of man.

The idea of a man "living by Fortune" congers up images of some lonely baccarat player who daily wagers the same ten dollars on the same number, and when he wins, he eats, and when he loses, he goes hungry. However, Fortune claims everything as her own with the singular exception of a man's soul. Only the soul is beyond the reach of Fortune. A man "lives by Fortune" when anything other than virtue gives his life meaning. "Living by Fortune" is thus not simply a dangerous way of living. The Lady equates it with idolatry.

Few Christians would claim to love anyone or anything more than God; however, the Lady is little interested in determining what is and is not an idol based merely on what we say. People say all manner of nice and flattering things about themselves. Rather, Lady Philosophy judges whether a man is an idolater by how he consoles himself in the midst of his suffering. While she never asks, the Lady must wonder how Boethius has dealt with being treated unfairly in the past. Surely this is not the first instance in his life in which he has been mistreated. His wife must have, at some point or another, lost her temper with him over nothing at all. Or else he was punished as a child for breaking a vase he never actually touched.

Many Americans demand some form of consolation for even the mildest forms of suffering. When a man is bored at work by ten in the morning and he knows the day is not likely to improve before dinner, he promises himself a stiff gin and tonic when he gets home. When a student is bored at school, or slaving to write an essay, he makes a vow to himself of something pleasant later on, the thought of which pulls him through his disinterest in whatever mundane thing is before him. When Fortune takes our pleasant things from us, we console ourselves with thoughts of pleasant things we can seize later on. If the suffering of work or school is made tolerable by thoughts of drink or television later, we live towards drink and television. Drink and television are the final things, the things which give value and meaning to our present ills. The week is made tolerable by the weekend. Fidelity is made tolerable by conjugality. Sobriety is made tolerable by inebriation. Work is made tolerable by pleasure.

Let us admit, though, that we are prone to overcompensating ourselves for our suffering. If a man is bored at work by ten in the morning and accordingly promises himself two good swigs from a bottle of gin the moment he gets through the door, as his day gets worse, he will often promise himself greater volumes of gin. While the pleasures men promise themselves to make their suffering tolerable are not always vicious, they often involve some form of oblivion, like liquor, drugs, or pornography.

Before delivering a test on Fridays, I often poll my students about their plans for the weekend, and there are usually two or three young men who say, "I am going to watch television all day on Saturday." These young men are also the ones who most shamelessly complain about school. While nine hours of television may not be as deleterious to the body as nine shots of bourbon, I have reservations about saying it is safer for the soul. We have all heard of high-functioning drunks; I doubt we know any high-functioning TV addicts. In the last several years, many men who have committed cataclysmic acts of violence against crowds of strangers have left behind documents revealing their final plans were a long time in the making. These men have suffered the rejection of women, getting cut off in traffic, long lines at the bank, noisy neighbors, and high heating bills for years, and the agitation they felt all the while was quelled by the thought of someday indulging in the ultimate act of oblivion, the murder of strangers and then suicide. When Dr. Jekyll tires of his work, he promises himself time spent as Hyde late at night, wandering the streets, killing men and assaulting girls with perfect anonymity. The promise of oblivion in the future allows us a foretaste here and now, and so a man tells himself, "If I can just make it until five this evening…"

Unless we are willing, from time to time, to deprive ourselves of the material consolations of Fortune, we will not find our final consolation in God much of a consolation at all. For the man who has endured every form of present suffering by promising himself food or drink or sex later on, the death bed will prove a profoundly disorienting place. The man who has spent his life looking forward to physical pleasure is bereft of direction in his final hours before death. "At least you will go to be with God," say his friends, and the man finds little solace in this idea, for going to God means leaving all the things he has loved most. Anticipating communion with God in the life to come requires practice now, habituation, and the only way to practice caring more about God than Fortune is to voluntarily reject Fortune. Of course, it is not as though finding consolation in God is merely a prospect for the life to come. I still lucidly recall the moment four years ago when I came home from church, directly poured myself a drink, and realized that I not only required the consolations of Fortune to make it through the work week,

I demanded consolation for going to church, as well. I have consoled myself with better turns of Fortune since I was a little child, and a man does not suddenly begin enjoying church or looking forward to worship just because he is old enough to have a mortgage.

Often I have heard Americans comfort themselves in their impiety by claiming, "Heaven is not going to be like some eternal church service." Given the variety of church services that exist, perhaps the claim has a modicum of merit. As an Orthodox Christian, granted, I do not believe Heaven will be like an eternal Methodist worship service. However, if I have even a shred of genuine conviction in the dogmatic claims my church makes about itself, I do believe Heaven will be like an eternal Divine Liturgy of St. John Chrysostom, the service offered to God every Sunday morning. So, too, the Methodist must conduct his life as though the eternity he looks forward to is none-too-crudely mirrored in what he says, hears, and smells on Sunday morning. The average man who justifies his disinterest in God with, "Heaven will not be like some eternal church service" does not want Heaven to be anything like a church service at all, ever. He has heard that Heaven is "the wedding feast of the Lamb," and so he white knuckles it through the hymns and sermon and when he gets home, he dines sumptuously and sighs with relief while forking up choice cuts of mutton that "Heaven will be more like this. Hell will be an eternal church service, with no decent lunch afterwards." If a man has been to church and does not think Heaven will be much like it, he should either find a church whose worship bears a closer resemblance to Heaven, or else he ought to quit going to church altogether and just do that thing which he thinks most heavenly. If Heaven is really "more like an eternal wedding feast" than a church service, then epicureanism or hedonism are far more fitting religions, for they better mirror reality, given that God is reality itself.

The only real consolation, Lady Philosophy teaches, is faith and hope and love of God. For the Christian, every consolation delivered to a man in the full bloom of health must contain the seed of death bed consolation. Four years ago, my wife became mysteriously ill and suffered from joint pain, stomach pain, fatigue, and all the anxieties which predictably come from such physical maladies. She received a battery of diagnoses, most of which required her to alter her diet, and foods she had enjoyed her entire life were suddenly prohibited. On one occasion, having realized that yet another diagnosis and drug regimen was not working, I began to wonder if she would simply live with such pain for the rest of her life. Perhaps this was not a stage she was passing through, but a new reality into which she was only just settling. I could offer her no promise of something pleasant, for pleasant things were slowly receding from her. "Well," I said to her, "at least you will be dead someday." While such words might strike healthy men as needlessly morose, Lady Philosophy insists the only genuine consolation in suffering is willing and grateful endurance that God might repay our virtue in the life to come. It takes a unique sort of man to suffer through a tough day of work, have a bottle of gin waiting for him at home, and yet to say, "At least I shall be dead someday," arrive home, skip the liquor and go to bed early and sober. And yet living this way, at least from time to time, is exactly what the Lady means when she refers to the "mutability" of Fortune. Fortune may take away liquor and money and the prettiness of a young wife, but Fortune cannot take away the day of death.

"Bad fortune, I think, is more use to a man than good fortune. Good fortune always seems to bring happiness, but deceives you with her smiles, whereas bad fortune is always truthful because by change she shows her true fickleness. Good fortune deceives, but bad fortune enlightens."

- Lady Philosophy, 2.8 (p. 44)

Bad luck is better than good luck. Good fortune is bad, but bad fortune is good. The man who tries his hardest and fails is better off than the man who tries his hardest and succeeds. I am not content this constitutes Lady Philosophy's most difficult teaching, although it is the idea which prompted the authoring of this narrow volume.

Several years ago, I attended a dinner wherein everyone was asked to anonymously submit a resolution to be debated over the meal. I submitted a paraphrase of Lady Philosophy's claim about good luck, although I hung it on the subject of sports. It is better to play your hardest and lose than to play your hardest and win. When read aloud by the moderator, the table met the claim with mild disdain. "If someone only ever loses, he will just become bitter," said one fellow. Everyone agreed. Several minutes of tepid back and forth followed, then the next resolution was read and we moved on. The odds were not really in favor of the paraphrased proverb gathering much traction. After all, it had been lifted from its context in a canonized piece of literature and released like a balloon on a windy day.

Nonetheless, days later I was still puzzling over the benign way the claim was dismissed. I had also lately seen a handful of lucidly reasoned essays online get lambasted in the comments section with banal hypothetical counterexamples, first impressions, and far-fetched what ifs. The modern man likes to imagine himself as a breaker of proverbs, a destroyer of maxims, a debunker of sages. If the modern man had a reasonable standard for debunking sages, his conversation would be tolerable. However, the modern man tends to assume that proverbs are like scientific laws and that a single counterexample effectively invalidates a theory.

If someone on social media says, "Do not drive drunk," someone will invariably reply, "Actually, my uncle was drunk the evening his wife went into labor and he lives forty miles out in the country. It was very sudden. The baby's umbilical cord was wrapped around its neck and my aunt didn't know this, but she could tell something was wrong, so she told my uncle he had to drive her to the hospital immediately. It would have taken an ambulance half an hour just to get to the house, which is out in the middle of the country. My uncle had started on a pint of cognac around six in the evening, and he finished it by eight o'clock, which is when my aunt said she didn't feel well. He drove her into town, but he can barely remember it now because he was so drunk at the time. The next day the doctor said my aunt was ten minutes away from dying the moment they wheeled her into the ER. If my uncle didn't drive her drunk, she would have died and so would have the baby. So I guess what you mean to say is, 'Usually it is best to not drive drunk,' or, 'Typically, driving drunk is a bad idea.' But you can't say 'Do not drive drunk,' or, 'Never drive drunk,' because if my uncle had not driven drunk, my cousin Jennifer would have never been born."

The modern man wants every ancient proverb qualified with words like "usually," "typically," "generally," "often," and "sometimes." He does not believe there is a way things are. He does not even believe there is a way things tend to be. Rather, he views the world as a series of accidents and arbitrary events. Every thing and every person in the world is atomized, isolated in its being, sequestered off from the habits of existence. Reality has no contours; being has no grooves. The modern man does not believe women are a certain way. He does not believe men are a certain way. He does not believe children or kings, farmers or prostitutes are a certain way. He believes that every human being alive is at war with the past, at war with tradition, and thus the modern man believes every farmer is reinventing farming, every king reinventing dominion, every woman reinventing femininity. Because every farmer is reinventing farming and every woman is reinventing femininity, the terms "woman" and "farmer" are empty. We should not expect the zeitgeist to be content until every weighty word in the dictionary has been gutted.

However, neither Solomon nor Christ qualified their proverbs, which is a fact vexing to both the literalist and the liberal. Throughout the book of Proverbs, Solomon describes the life of "the evil man" and "the righteous man" without qualification. "Whoever works his land will have plenty of bread, but he who follows worthless pursuits will have plenty of poverty," claims Solomon in Proverbs 28:19. Solomon does not claim that whoever works his land "will usually have plenty of bread," simply that he "will have plenty." Neither does he claim that a man who follows worthless pursuits "will typically be poor," just that he'll be poor.

The book of Proverbs is full of claims about lazy men starving, righteous men thriving, and adulterers getting slaughtered before their time, but the modern man has heard a story somewhere about a lazy man who won the lottery, a righteous man who was hated by his neighbors, and an adulterer who took his secret to the grave at the ripe old age of ninety-two. The modern man wants every proverb qualified, asterisked, and stated so tentatively that it has nothing to do with himself. Only a common man cares about what commonly happens, but ours is a generation of proud weirdos. For a proverb to be of value to a man, he must be see himself as normal, ordinary, common. He must not see himself as special, atypical, excused from the law of averages. A proverb is not a law, but a description of the world right down the middle. Thus, the more unique a man thinks himself, the less open he is to the wisdom of the ages, for Solomon is not interested in describing unusual cases, but conventional ones. Receiving the wisdom of a proverb requires humility, for a man must lay down his right to claim himself as exceptional. He must see himself as the kind of person for whom morality tales and warning labels were written.

Solomon's wisdom was indebted to the perspective which came with his kingly power. People in positions of power are more apt to see the world as a place where things tend to work a certain way. Powerful people who govern hundreds or thousands of lives simply do not have the time to govern each man individually, and so they must see the world in terms of averages and tendencies. A good king governs his people, not his individuals. To a lesser extent, teachers also see the world in terms of tendencies. Every school year, a high school teacher is responsible for the spiritual well-being of fifty children. This is far more children than the average parent is responsible for, even if the responsibility of the teacher for a certain child does not run as deep as that of the child's father. The high school teacher sees the eighth-grade boys smirk when a benign use of the word "ejaculate" passes in *Paradise Lost*, but one of the boys' mother insists her son has no idea what sex even is. A teacher will insist a certain girl's test work has all the tell-tale signs of being copied from the boy beside her, but the girl's mother will insist this is a wild coincidence. Rookie teachers are amazed when students lie to get out of doing their homework; veteran teachers know that "foolishness is bound up in the heart" of baptized and unbaptized children alike. The most productive parent-teacher conferences begin with father and mother asking, "What are we doing wrong?" The least productive conferences begin with, "You have probably noticed my daughter is very smart," or, "My son is very special." When I hear such claims, I always want to hand the parent a class list and say, "If you could circle the names of the students who are less special than your daughter, that would be helpful."

As the chief of sinners, I acknowledge that all warnings, all cautions, all statistics, all proverbs and maxims apply doubly for myself. I am not one to tell myself, "I will never get divorced. Divorce is not possible for me, for I truly love my wife." Given how normal I am, and given how normal divorce is, I could very easily get divorced. If I want to avoid getting divorced, a great effort is required on my part to rise above the commonness of my own soul. I am sufficiently intimidated by prescription drugs which come with labels which read, "May cause suicidal thoughts." The fact that I can explain platonic metaphysics and the more esoteric claims of St. Athanasius's *On the Incarnation* by no means excuses me from such warnings. Rather, such knowledge helps me take those warnings seriously.

But let us return to the subject at hand.

Good luck is at war with the *memento mori*, the knowledge of the certainty of death, and when things are going well for a man, he forgets that he will someday die. When I am sick, I confess my sins. When I recover, I return to my sins. When my pockets are full of cash and my wife is flirtatious and I have just ordered a good drink, the pride of life swells in my heart and I forget God. I order a second drink. When I feel a mysterious pain in my side, and the money is spent, and my wife is cross, I repent of my sins.

To clarify this, I ask my students to consider the point writ large. Imagine two professional quarterbacks who enter the NFL at the same time. One quarterback goes four straight seasons without winning a game, the other goes four straight seasons without losing a game. One quarterback knows no loss, the other knows nothing but loss. The losing quarterback receives anonymous death threats on the phone every night from people in his own city, while the winning quarterback never pays for a meal, for everyone in his city is desperate to show their love. Which one of these men would prove more interesting to talk to for an hour? Which of these men makes the better husband? If neither of these men were Christians, which man would be more likely to convert? Which one of these men responds more reasonably when he does not get his way?

To such questions, the modern man is always eager to say, "But what if the only reason the losing quarterback keeps playing is that he is desperate to win? What if the losing quarterback is bitter and it's the bitterness that drives him? What if the winning quarterback's secret is his disinterest in winning? What if the winning quarterback feels a power not his own coursing through his body—and what if the only thing which separates this man from giving his life to God is someone telling him where his power ultimately comes from? What if the losing quarterback despises God, and blames God for being stingy with glory?" None of these suggestions is illogical, but neither is the story about a drunk uncle driving his pregnant wife to the hospital. On the other hand, when rich young quarterbacks behave like selfish fools, no one is terribly surprised. When a rich young quarterback conducts himself with dignity, humility, and quietude, he is a perplexing marvel.

The modern man feigns confusion at the young ruler who was told to sell all he had and "went away sorrowful, for he had great possessions" (Matt. 19:22), and he is equally confused by the fact that the rich man in the Parable of Lazarus and the rich man is a "rich man." The ultimate head-scratcher is the woe Christ pronounces on "you who are rich, for you have received your consolation." However, lest this book merely become a footnote to the works of Stanley Hauerwas and John Howard Yoder, I should say that I have little interest in condemning those who have a lot of money. I champion the political ideals of Sir Edmund Burke, and no man in the last five hundred years has put as mystical and theological a spin on hordes of money quite like the father of conservative political philosophy. A great many wealth apologists prefer "Blessed are the poor in spirit" to "Blessed are the poor" because they are content that everyone from Rockefeller to Fitzwilliam Darcy obtained a sort of poverty through generosity and humility. I confess I find the former iteration of the beatitude far more disconcerting than the latter. If a man could obtain blessedness through mere lack of funds, salvation is for sale and Simon Magus had the right idea in Acts 8, but simply did not offer the apostles enough money for the Holy Spirit.

On this point, we can turn to one of the most disconcerting moments in *The Consolation*, which is Boethius's self-defense. Having listened to Lady Philosophy dismiss the pleasant effects of Fortune, Boethius tells her he was "little…governed by worldly ambition," but rather "sought the means of engaging in politics so that virtue should not grow old unpraised" (p. 40). Lady Philosophy is unimpressed with Boethius's claims, though, and replies that his work is typical of "natural excellence" (p. 41) but that his mind is "not yet perfected with the finishing touch of complete virtue" (p. 41). Once the implications of this little exchange are understood, the average American Christian should be sufficiently offended.

Boethius and Philosophy are not arguing about Boethius's salvation, at least not so far as the word "salvation" passes in conversation today. *The Consolation* is a conversation between a saved man and his mentor. Lady Philosophy is not trying to bring Boethius to Christ. Boethius's frustration will not be solved by saying the sinner's prayer, and neither did Boethius's problems begin with his unfair sentence and incarceration. Rather, Boethius is a man who, despite being a saved and born-again Christian, nonetheless committed his life to rather pedestrian affairs of earthly glory. Boethius's problem isn't that he's not a Christian, but that he's not a very good person. The Lady's suggestion that Boethius was driven by a desire for earthly glory touches a nerve, and Boethius shrinks back from the Lady's conversation to defend himself. Boethius believes, as do most American Christians, that the need to be heavenly-minded is a problem for other people. Boethius wants to say:

I did the best I could. I have fallen short, but who hasn't? Despite the ways I have fallen short, I have kept the fire of human goodness burning a little longer. I have not been depraved or cowardly. I am not the problem. The problem with the world is that it is filled with wicked men, and if more people would behave reasonably and care less for pleasure, the world would be a fine place to live.

So, too, when I ask my students who is most to blame for the problems with the world, they often say "lukewarm Christians" or "nominal Christians." When I ask what this means, I am told that lukewarm Christians are those who attend church but are not fully committed to God. Lukewarm Christians adopt the postures and prejudices of Christianity, but cave to all manner of vice— vulgarity, licentiousness, drug use, crudity, perversity. On the other hand, students who smoke, curse, do drugs, and watch horror movies are more apt to say that "lukewarm Christians" are the ones who are overly performing their piety and simply cannot admit their faults. Mild Christians believe mediocrity derives from easily observable vices, while wild Christians think lukewarmth derives from vices more easily hidden, like pride and arrogance. Theology-buff Presbyterians are more apt to condemn garden variety Baptists and Methodists as nominal. Protestants condemn Christmas-and-Easter Catholics as nominal. Pentecostals identify dull liturgies as the mark of nominalism.

One of the greatest tricks the Devil ever pulled was convincing American Christians that the real problem with the world is *out there*. As soon as nominal Christianity is thought of as a thing *out there*, the Christianity in a man's heart necessarily becomes the barometer for measuring authentic spirituality. If a man reads his Bible and prays four times a week, the "nominal Christians" out there are the ones who read it less. If a man reads his Bible and prays three times a week, the "nominal Christians" read it less. A man is forever left assuming there is a massive contingent of Christians in the world who do less than he does—regardless of how much he does—and he condemns them for their disinterest in God. Condemning the nominalism out there leads us to believe that our own efforts are always sufficient, always real, no matter what they are. The problem is not that a man believes he is saved "by faith alone," but that he thinks whatever he is doing is faith, or that his disinterest in doing anything at all is what constitutes his faith. Spiritual struggle is pointless.

At the same time, the man who condemns most of the Christian population for doing too little is also vaguely aware that some Christians do more than he does. Should this make him feel guilty? Should this bring his soul to a place of humility? Should he please himself less and serve others more, inspired by the likes of a Mother Theresa or a Francis of Assisi? No, of course not, for he is free to tell himself, "Anyone who does more than I do is simply trying to earn their salvation by works. My piety is expertly calibrated for enjoyment of this world and the next world. Any less piety and I could not enjoy the next life, any more piety and I could not enjoy this life. When I arrive at the Great Judgment, the Judge will say, Well done, thou careful and prudent quasihedonist."

Most American Christians are content to hear preachers talk about cultivating virtue only to the point the sermon begins to sting. When a sermon stings, we accuse the minister of preaching "works righteousness." We condemn unbelievers for their lack of virtue, but any lack of virtue in Christians is capably dealt with by the good works of Christ. A lack of good works is problematic for unbelievers, but a lack of good works is insignificant for Christians, who simply draft on the merits of Jesus. Christianity is not principally a religion of faith, hope, and love, but a religion for people who are tired of feeling guilty for never having faith, hope, and love, and only marginally interested in doing anything about it. Of course, a classical education is not much interested in "salvation" as the term is typically employed today. Salvation is not the ease of a life well-lived, but the beginning of something arduous. Consider Christ's interaction with the rich ruler in Luke 18:

> ...*a ruler asked him, "Good Teacher, what must I do to inherit eternal life?" And Jesus said to him, "Why do you call me good? No one is good except God alone. You know the commandments: 'Do not commit adultery, Do not murder, Do not steal, Do not bear false witness, Honor your father and mother.'" And he said, "All these I have kept from my youth." When Jesus heard this, he said to him, "One thing*

you still lack. Sell all that you have and distribute to the poor, and
you will have treasure in Heaven; and come, follow me." But when
he heard these things, he became very sad, for he was extremely rich.

Attentive readers will note that Christ does not answer the ruler's question. The ruler asks how he may "inherit eternal life," but Christ responds by giving instruction on what he must do to "have treasure in Heaven." In like fashion, Lady Philosophy has little interest in showing Boethius how to inherit anything, but how to store up, how to strive, how to run, how to do. The threat of Hell has as little place in *The Consolation* as it does in Christ's interaction with the rich ruler, for the Lady is speaking to a friend of God who is simply a little hazy on Who God is and what God offers.

Since becoming a teacher, I have often found my students are resistant to the idea of storing up treasure in heaven, although this owes not to their youth, but the Christian milieu of America. While we are not opposed to the idea of virtue or the concept of treasure in heaven, we are just a little offended by the idea that treasure may be stored up or that virtue may be cultivated. Occasionally, students tell me treasure in heaven may not be intentionally stored up, for this is selfish. Rather, virtue is the kind of thing a man accidentally runs into. A man may only ever possess heavenly treasure haphazardly, unintentionally, arbitrarily, for grace is free and the very notion of striving for grace ruins grace.

I first encountered this aversion to pursue virtue years ago while teaching Dante's *Purgatorio*. As I am not Catholic, and neither were any of my students at the time, I warned my students against dismissing the Purgatorio simply because the title made reference to an exclusively Catholic doctrine. "You will notice," I told them, "that Mount Purgatory is a place on earth. *Purgatorio* is an account of life on earth, an account of sanctification, of sin being purged from a man's soul." Any initial fears that the book would prove a waste of time subsided quickly and everyone began reading with an open mind. But the further in the book we read, the more pronounced their hesitation became.

Dante's Mount Purgatory is a place where men ardently strive for the virtue which answers the vice typical of their former lives. The glutton must fast, the slothful must run, the proud must humble themselves, the lustful must burn unconsumed. Slowly but surely, my students moved from suspicion to outright hostility.

"This is salvation by works," they said.

"No. Everyone in *Purgatory* is already saved," I replied.

"Then what do they need to work for?"

"They are working to become good."

"Yes, that is salvation by works," someone said, and a few others agreed.

"What if I said they were storing up treasure in Heaven?" I asked.

"If they are only doing the good works to store up treasure in heaven, then they are laboring selfishly," my students replied.

Ever since this interaction, I have made it a point of asking every class I teach about treasure in heaven. Some students are sympathetic to the idea, but the average student confesses little interest. Storing up treasure in heaven is allowable, but not necessary. The man who struggles to store up treasure in heaven stores up none, for he labors selfishly. Why do good works, then? I am typically told that we should seek virtue because Christ died for us, not because virtue has any value in and of itself. I have pressed my students to justify this position.

I say, "But Christ commands us to store up treasure in heaven. In the Sermon on the Mount, Christ tells His followers not to store up treasure on earth, where moth and rust destroy, but to store up treasure in heaven, where the treasure will not fade and cannot be stolen. Is this not a command? Christ says, 'Store up treasure . . .' and does that not sound like, 'Thou shalt not steal'? Isn't it an imperative statement? And if Christ tells us to do something, shouldn't we be intentional about it?

Should we not plan how to do it? Strategize?" At this point, students have asked for clarification.

"What," they ask, "do you think treasure in heaven is?"

I reply, "Christ's remark about storing up treasure in heaven comes at the end of His teachings about piety in Matthew 6. When you give alms… When you pray… When you fast… Fasting, praying, and alms-giving are the three great pillars of piety, the three great acts of faith. Christ is instructing His followers how to be pious. No one can repay the giving of alms but God. No one can answer prayer but God. No one can reward a fast but God. All three of these are acts of faith rendered unto God, not unto men. Man can only repay with the things of man, and the things of man can be stolen by thieves and destroyed by vermin. It is foolish to labor for man, Christ teaches, because the rewards of man are ephemeral, fading. An act of faith can only be repaid by God and God repays with the ultimate boon, communion with Himself. The man who performs works of piety stores up treasure in heaven, and in heaven, God will reward that faith with His own life."

"That," my students reply, "is salvation by works, for who would want to go to heaven if they did not have any treasure stored up there?"

Until a teacher addresses the fact that many students simply do not believe it is necessary to cultivate virtue, *The Consolation* will merely be an exercise in condemning other people, and so will the whole of a liberal arts education.

As I have mentioned elsewhere, there are two Boethiuses in *The Consolation*. There is the character of Boethius who speaks with Lady Philosophy and there is Boethius the author, who has written Lady Philosophy into existence. When Boethius the character recoils at the suggestion that he has not lived a life of profound virtue, but a mundane life characterized by the pursuit of men's praise, we should step back from Boethius the character and see the oblique strategies of Boethius the author in teaching virtue. The author's critique of the character is, in fact, a critique of himself. As he nears the end of his life, Boethius the author tips his hand to readers and suggests that even though he has the wisdom to write a book like *The Consolation*, he has not been faithful in living by everything he knows to be true. Sitting on death row, the author experiences great pangs of remorse and anger that his life is coming to an abrupt end at the age of forty-four, but he also knows that his philosophical commitments do not permit him such anger. He has failed to entirely live by the principles he teaches, and he admits as much.

The classical teacher must do the same. The only way of jarring students out of a state of moral complacency is for the teacher to admit his own faults, his own mediocrity. The same students who believe the problem with the world is all the mediocre Christians out there also generally believe that adults are naturally good people. This unresolvable contradiction thus sits at moral center of the teenager's intellectual universe:

I am sufficiently Christian
and
I will be actually good when I become an adult.

Students have not only promised themselves they will read the Bible and pray more as adults, but generally believe that a surplus of power and money will alleviate the need to lie and that the acquisition of a wife or husband will suddenly quench the crushing desire for sex or approval from which they suffer. Teenagers and adults both maintain a secret body of knowledge from the other, though teenagers live in far greater fear of being found out. This secret body of knowledge (who has smoked what, touched who, cheated on which tests) creates an anxiety which the teenager believes will disappear in adulthood, for as adults, they will no longer live in fear of being found out. Once they no longer fear being found out, life will become simple and peaceful. Teenagers generally believe that adults are good people, even the adults they do not like. Having tried reading the Bible, teenagers know that piety is a somewhat dull affair, but adults have dull tastes, so virtue and piety come naturally to adults. Church is a bit tedious, but so is James Taylor, and wine has a disgusting flinty flavor, but to a grown man, all three are suitably appealing.

What is more, adults preach rather simple lessons about the value of reading the Bible and praying. If adults are so insistent that prayer and Scripture are necessary to peace, surely they practice what they preach. The teenager is tone deaf to the regret, embarrassment, and self-loathing which attend most adult lives. The teenager is worried about finding a decent spouse, a decent job, a respectable house and car. Most students who attend classical schools live in families wherein these things are a given, hence most students believe their parents have succeeded in life. If a father's chief concerns for his children are good grades and a good college, he reinforces the idea that virtue is a hobby suitable to a man's retirement years, but not a necessity before then.

Because teenagers believe adults are good, teenagers perceive most moral advice as self-serving. Adults are not teaching goodness, but their own simple way of life. The teenager rightly understands that he may presently waste away his reputation and regain it later. A teenager caught smoking a joint in the men's room can make a full social recovery in a matter of months. A teacher caught doing the same may never make a full social recovery. The teenager lacks a pressing material reason to be good, whereas the adult does not.

If the teacher is to disabuse his students of the idea that people necessarily become good as they age, he must rouse them from their settled opinion that adults are naturally good, or that virtue inevitably follows old age. Like Boethius, the teacher must reveal his own mediocrity to his students. He must show his students that he is not a good person.

In Book IV, Chapter 4 of *De Doctrina Christiana*, St. Augustine describes the roll of the teacher as such:

> *It is the duty, then, of the interpreter and teacher of Holy Scripture, the defender of the true faith and the opponent of error, both to teach*

what is right and to refute what is wrong, and in the performance
of this task to conciliate the hostile, to rouse the careless, and to tell
the ignorant both what is occurring at present and what is probable
in the future. But once his hearers are friendly, attentive, and ready
to learn, whether he has found them so, or has himself made them so
the remaining objects are to be carried out in whatever way the case
requires. If the hearers need teaching, the matter treated of must be
made fully known by means of narrative. On the other hand, to clear
up points that are doubtful requires reasoning and the exhibition
of proof. If, however, the hearers require to be roused rather than
instructed, in order that they may be diligent to do what they al-
ready know, and to bring their feelings into harmony with the truths
they admit, greater vigor of speech is needed. Here entreaties and
reproaches, exhortations and upbraidings, and all the other means of
rousing the emotions, are necessary.

The good teacher rarely upbraids his students. The good teacher upbraids himself. The good teacher confesses that he cares too much for
the things of the world, as did Boethius. I am a lukewarm, mediocre,
nominal Christian. I tell my students this as early in the year as possible. I do not want them thinking me something I am not. I tell them,
"When you think of lukewarm Christianity, think of me. I go to church,
but I am not fully committed to God. I have been confessing the same
sins for twenty years. I do not tithe ten percent. I am one of *those people.*
You will sometimes hear people complaining about 'all the hypocrites in
church.' I am one of those hypocrites. I do not enjoy church. I feel very
good when church is over, but I am often checking my watch during the
service itself. I do not read my Bible very often. I have given up making
excuses. I do not read my Bible because I do not want to read it, and I
do not want to read it because I am not a very good person. I pray very
earnestly when I am sick and I forget about God once I get better." Giv-
en that I am an adult who has achieved a respectable job, income, and an

automobile, many students are quite shocked to hear all this.

However, after the shock passes, students experience relief. The teacher who confesses his faults is no longer speaking the separate language of adults, but a universal human language of guilt, hope, and longing. The confessional teacher opens himself up to be judged by his books. Boethius judges himself, and in so doing, he paves a way for his students to do the same. Students are afraid to judge themselves according to the moral demands of Boethius simply because no one has shown them how to do it. If the teacher uses the text to condemn his students, his students will simply learn to use the text to condemn their peers. But when the teacher submits himself to the difficult teachings of a moral philosopher and shows all the ways he is lacking, his students come to see a man may admit failure and live to tell of it. All things by example. All things by imitation. While a good teacher is a good storyteller, the good teacher is also a performer, for he must show his students how Boethius is painful to read. This is something quite different than saying, "When I first read Boethius, I found it very convicting." Rather, *The Consolation* must be convicting today, now, even as the teacher reads it aloud and teaches it. If the teacher wants *The Consolation* to change his students, *The Consolation* must change the teacher. The students must see it happen, not be aware that it happened in the safety of the past, wherein the teacher may vaguely allude to his "former imperfections." The teacher should not be concerned with making himself the laughing stock of his students, but should embrace his role as a comedian, a whipping boy, a Christ figure who does not suffer on behalf of others, but as an example to others who are then told to take up their crosses.

Teaching *The Consolation* from a confessional standpoint will charge discussions of the book with verve and rescue the book from the "cold slumber of vulgarity," as C.S. Lewis put it, typical of students who retreat to "salvation" whenever moral teaching becomes weighty, convicting, and uncomfortable. If sin actually makes a man miserable, a decent teacher should be able to prove the point from stories taken from his own life as well as the lives of others. Sin makes saved people miserable. My sin makes me miserable. I have also seen saved people who love Jesus destroy the lives of their children through selfishness and ignorance. I have seen saved people become addicted to liquor and pornography. I have seen saved people lead other saved people into poverty, debt, and loneliness. I have seen saved people betray other saved people. Saved people kill other saved people in wars on a regular basis. The American Civil War was fought between saved people, as was the Revolutionary War, the Thirty Years' War and the Hundred Years' War. I have been shouted at by saved people, lied about by saved people, and on several occasions saved people have gone after my job because they hated me that much. We are vaguely aware that someone in the Bible said something about good works being "filthy rags," although we are not sure who said it, where it was said, to whom it was said, what the context was, or what the Church made of the claim for the first thousand years of Christian history. However, the fact that someone somewhere said good works are like "filthy rags" means we are free to console ourselves like a tribe of nihilists. Having accepted a cheap, easy, modern American understanding of "saved by faith," it is possible for a saved man to move through the world recklessly destroying the happiness of others, inflicting pain and misery on helpless children, spoiling the imaginations of adolescents, preying upon the vulnerabilities of women, and tempting friends to vice and malice, all without ever needing to worry about anything worse than breaking a few hearts and inspiring a few tears.

But if a man won't go to Heaven for giving to the poor, then neither will he go to hell for stealing from the poor. If a man won't go to heaven for being chaste, then neither will he go to Hell for frittering his twenties away looking at internet pornography. Having reduced salvation to a legal decision, and having reduced that legal decision to nothing more than tepid consent, the long history of Christian philosophy, Scripture, ethics, pastoral theology, and homiletics can be reduced to a feeling, a warm undulation of the heart called "faith," which takes place somewhere in the deep recesses of the human heart. My claim is not that humans were good prior to the twentieth century, but that they felt a little guilty for the right reasons.

While Machiavelli taught that efficient rulers make their own good luck, Boethius teaches that virtue means making your own bad luck. In Christ's parable, Abraham tells the rich man in Hell that he had his good things "in your lifetime," and the virtuous man hastens to bad things. When he wants a drink, he goes thirsty. When he wants to defend himself, he is silent. When he wants to sleep, he rises early to pray. When he wants time to himself, he seeks out the lonely. He assumes the role of the dead man, to whom physical comfort is cut off. He does not console himself with certainty of his own salvation, but daily approaches the Lord with hope and fear and asks, *Good teacher, what must I do to be saved?*

CHAPTER FOUR

Temptation and Besetting Sins

"It is nothing serious, only a touch of amnesia that he
is suffering, the common disease of deluded minds.
He has forgotten for a while who he is, but he will
soon remember once he has recognized me."

- Lady Philosophy, 1.2 (p. 6)

After telling Boethius that he is "sick" in the first chapter, the
Lady offers a more particular diagnosis in the second. Boethius has "amnesia," and "has forgotten who he is" (p. 6). While
Boethius has received a rich education in philosophy, readers of *The
Consolation* who are newcomers to philosophical literature should
not feel alienated. Any Christian who has received a rudimentary
education in the Faith has the same knowledge of wisdom which
the Lady assumes Boethius has forgotten. God is man's friend and
the lover of his soul. God is all good, and He works every event
and accident of a man's life together for his salvation, if only a man
retains a seed of love for God. So long as a man knows this, every
kind of sin is amnesia. The Lady's assessment of sin as amnesia is
not true on a theological level or a philosophical level. Her claim is
eminently pastoral.

While all sin involves self-forgetting, the idea is most easily illustrated and understood with a certain kind of sin, the besetting sin. A

besetting sin is not a sin a man commits occasionally. A besetting sin is a sin a man commits every day. A certain man might steal something but once a year. For all his problems, he is not tempted to take what does not belong to him, and referring to this man as "a thief" makes little sense, for even if he is painfully honest with himself, he cannot remember the last thing he stole. The Devil is cunning and knows there is little point in attacking a man where he is strong. However, the non-thief in question does have a terrible weakness for liquor and the devil has an impressive track record of successfully tempting the man to drunkenness at least four or five nights a week. Drunkenness is his besetting sin.

A man's besetting sin is the sin he thinks of when he hears the word "sin." When the priest refers to "sin," the glutton thinks only of gluttony. When the lecher reads St. Paul describe "bondage to decay," he thinks only of lust. The glutton and the lecher commit sins other than gluttony and drunkenness, though they experience little guilt for these sins. They are not crushed beneath the weight of these sins. On the rare occasion the lecher has too much to drink, he confesses his sin the morning after, accepts forgiveness, and gets on with the day. When the glutton is at the hardware store and does not feel like waiting twenty minutes in line to buy just one nail, he pockets the nail, and the next day has nearly forgotten all about his thieving—or else he returns to the store, ashamedly pays for the nail, and does not steal anything else for many years. We accept forgiveness for occasional sins, for we do not know when we will commit them again.

We tend to find it much harder to accept forgiveness for our besetting sins, though, because we cannot conceive of going a day without them. A man confesses his besetting sin and before the words have left his lips, he already knows he will make the same confession on the following evening after caving to the same temptation once again. Consider the lecher in the moments after he caves to temptation. He feels foolish, ashamed. He beholds his face in a mirror and tells himself that he must remember this shame when he is tempted again. He tells himself that the pleasure gained from his vice is simply not worth the stinging remorse which immediately sets in afterwards. Nonetheless, the following day, the Devil goes back to work and whispers one of two things in the lecher's ear.

He might say, "The problem with last night was that you went entirely too far. Of course you were going to feel guilty when it was all said and done. I have not seen such immoderation in quite some time. The problem was not that you gave in to temptation, but that you gave into it with such severity, such reckless abandon. My word, even King Herod would have second guessed himself after such hedonism. What you want is a much milder yielding to pleasure. You want something temperate, something gentler on the stomach. Kinky, say, but not perverse."

Or else the Devil will say, "The problem with last night was that you did not go nearly far enough. You sinned enough to feel guilty, but not enough to feel much pleasure. That was boyish sinning, old friend! Simply tepid! Tonight, you need to sin like a man. With a little practice, you will see that the voice of conscience is no different than any other voice— it can be overpowered. You bought a ticket for sin, granted, but you did not get your money's worth. Make the remorse worth your while."

While the man remembers how ashamed he felt the last time he caved to temptation, a rival voice has begun telling him that he need not feel that shame again. The circumstances of the sin can be altered so that the shame is either sublimated by pleasure or else so trivial as to go unnoticed. The man spends his day contemplating another foray into his besetting sin, promising himself it will not be like last time. He received a bad exchange rate for his guilt on his last outing, and he has vowed to get a higher return tonight. The afternoon is spent finagling circumstances, recalculating and recalibrating.

In this planning, amnesia sets in. Remorse from the previous evening is forgotten in a frenzy of intellectual activity. It is in this moment of temptation that a man most desperately needs to recall his former shame, but the Devil has distracted him with a whole bevy of new tasks. The prying eyes of his wife must be circumnavigated, an excuse to leave the house must be invented, a plausible cover for the morning after must be settled on. Some men waste the best years of their lives strategizing ways to enjoy their vices apart from guilt. On the one hand, they quickly forget the good resolutions which attend their feelings of guilt ("I will never do it again…"), but on the other hand, they forget what it feels like to live apart from the crushing burden of guilt. As opposed to believing rightly that sin is a nothingness, a cancer, a man comes to believe that his sin is what he is, for it occupies so much of his time, his thought life, his wallet. Beneath the weight of his besetting sin, he comes to believe that life must be spent in a black cloud of shame; to live is to fear being found out. When he imagines life without his wife and children, he sees only an endless surrender to his besetting sin. While his wife is out of town, or he is out of town, his hours and days are devoured by a single temptation, a single vice. He comes to think of his besetting sin as his real self, his true self hidden beneath all the pretenses of fatherhood, career, and Christian conviction.

> **"Corrupted men sit throned on high;**
> **By strange reversal wickedness**
> **Downtreads the necks of holy men."**
> **- Boethius complains of the world, 1.5 (p. 16)**

M an is free to obey God, but he is also free to rebel. In his rebellion against God, man subjects himself to Fortune. Boethius' complaint that "Corrupted men sit throned on high" is no abstract meditation on the general unfairness of life, but a specific objection to the way his own life has played out. The Lady will wait until nearly the end of their conversation to finally put Boethius's objection against the injustice of the world to rest, and in the meantime, she listens with patience and begins administering the "gentler medicines" on Boethius' wounded mind. The first dosage of the gentler medicines concerns his exile. The man who loves God, the Lady suggests, can never be banished from his true home, for God is the true home of every man and God makes His home in the heart of those who love Him. The man who loves God can never be forced from his true home, for God does not depart from a man except the man sin, and no one can force another to sin. A man can reject God and escape Him, but only if he chooses to do so. Augustine teaches that after Adam rejects God, God calls to Adam, "Where are you?" to show Adam that they have been separated. God does not force the separation on Adam, but Adam willingly banishes himself from God. If a man makes his home on Earth, he invariably sets himself on a course for banishment, for he will ultimately die and his soul will depart earth to be judged by God. The man who fears earthly banishment can never live in peace, for his banishment is forthcoming, inevitable, perhaps coming to overtake him at this very moment. But the man who sees himself as an alien and sojourner on Earth is reminded his exile will end every time he suffers a little bad luck. Every lost wallet, every broken bone, every expensive car repair is a step toward God. On the day of his death, his banishment ends and he is welcomed into an eternal home. When bad luck is slow to come, asceticism can produce it on the fly. Asceticism is willing exile from Earth.

When I speak of asceticism here, I mean both the radical fasting of hermits and the vows of chastity which monks endure; however, merely closing your eyes to pray is also an act of asceticism, for it deprives the body of sight (in the same way fasting deprives the body of nourishment). The couple who waits until marriage to have sex has also willingly endured a deprivation of bodily pleasure. Mothers who tell their children, "No snacking. You'll spoil your dinner" are ascetics. Eating dessert last means waiting for the richest pleasures. Wrapping a gift and placing it under the Christmas tree in the middle of December similarly follows an ascetic logic, for doing so suggests that not all knowledge is immediately beneficial. Presbyterians and Lutherans might not approve of monasteries, but the principles of asceticism are simply necessary for a man to stay sane and healthy.

"And it is because you don't know the end and purpose of things that you think the wicked and criminal have power and happiness."
- Lady Philosophy, 1.6 (p. 20)

B oethius claims that God guides creation, but when the Lady asks Boethius how God guides creation towards His own ends, Boethius is lost. He says all things come from God, but he does not know "the end and purpose of things." The Lady is incredulous that he could know the genesis of a thing without also knowing its telos.

When the Lady suggests the wicked do not actually have power and happiness, she is relying on traditional Christian metaphysics. Before teaching *The Consolation*, or at very least before delving into Book 2, I find it helpful to give students a rough outline of basic Christian metaphysics. When the Lady suggests Boethius is delusional for believing that the wicked "have power," most students will need a little convincing. Do the wicked not obviously have power? Was the twentieth century not well populated with powerful dictators who slaughtered millions? Are there not bullies even in Christian schools who have the power to make life miserable for the weak?

Lady Philosophy connects power and happiness, though, because power as she refers to it here is not sheer physical strength (the ability to lift heavy things), but the capacity to satisfy one's desires. Power is the power to make oneself happy, content. The wicked do not have the power to satisfy their desires, or else in fulfilling their desires the wicked find they are not satisfied.

The Lady drafts on the Augustinian idea that evil is not an existent thing, but a non-existence. Evil is not a thing, but a nothing, an absence, a cancer, a lack. I often explain this concept to my students by asking them to consider the crack in the Liberty Bell.

"Is the crack in the Liberty Bell part of the Liberty Bell?" I ask, and if I am feeling generous I warn them in advance that there is a trick to the question.

"No," someone replies, although not out of conviction, but suspicion.

"Why?" I ask, and this question is harder to answer.

The crack is, after all, the most readily identifiable feature of the bell, so if the crack is not part of the bell, why do we identify the bell with the crack? After allowing students to mull over the question, I ask them what they would say if a friend reached into his jacket pocket, pulled out nothing, held out his empty hand and said, "For show and tell today, I brought the crack in the Liberty Bell." The claim is absurd, of course. My students respond, "The crack is where the bell is not. If it was part of the bell, the bell and the crack could be separated." This is true. The crack is the absence of the bell, the negation of the bell. On the other hand, if the crack were intended by the bell's maker, then inasmuch as the crack detracted from the bell's proper use, the evil would simply be in the mind of the maker. The crack is not what works in the bell, but what renders it useless. So, too, the power to tell a lie is not really a power, but an inability to tell the truth. The power to steal is not truly an ability, but an inability to be content with what God has already given. The power to lust is simply the inability to enjoy chastity.

Of course, temptation invariably presents itself as a genuine power, and thus many of my students think of sin as a genuine power which they are arbitrarily (and unreasonably) not permitted to use. Put another way, my students think of sin as counterfeit money which could be used to acquire real goods, although those real goods would be acquired through false means; the goods are real even if the money is not. When the Lady disparages Boethius's confidence that evil men are "powerful and happy," she has begun to question the idea that sin is analogous to counterfeit money.

Too often, we accept sin as it presents itself, and when we are tempted, sin commends itself to us as genuine salvation. Sin always presents itself as the lesser of two evils. Sin is a solution, not a problem. The Devil is not an idiot, after all. He never tells us to do what is wicked *because* it is wicked; he tells us to be wicked to avoid something worse.

Consider the young man who is sitting down to write an essay for school:

Devil: This essay would be much easier to write if you looked at a little pornography first.

Student: I need to get this thing done. It's due tomorrow. If I get started on pornography, I won't finish writing the essay.

Devil: Oh, that is simply not the case. Actually, if you don't look at pornography, you won't be able to finish this essay. You will try to write the essay, but you will continually be distracted by other desires. Just get it over with.

Student: It is wrong. I will feel guilty about it.

Devil: Maybe, but look, I am dealing in the realm of common sense. You will feel a little guilty about it, but you will finish your essay.

Student: I won't finish my essay. I will be angry with myself.

Devil: Even if that happens, which I doubt, feeling angry with yourself has never stopped you from finishing necessary work before, has it? You have certain desires. From time to time, those desires need to be satiated before you can invest your whole attention on some noble work. Who can say where those desires come from? The desires are there, nonetheless. You will not finish your essay if you keep pestering yourself with thoughts of lust. Giving in to lust is the only way to get around the distraction of lust and returning to your work. What is going to happen if you do not finish this essay?

Student: I will fail this class. My semester grade is on the line here.

Devil: Exactly. So you can spend ten minutes giving in to lust, or you can spend the rest of the evening trying to write this essay with the porn mosquito buzzing in your ear—which will mean failing the class. What is going to happen if you fail the class?

Student: My father will chew me out. I will have to take a class this summer.

Devil: If you fail this class, your transcripts are going to suffer. Your odds of getting a decent scholarship will take a hit. You need that scholarship to get into a decent college and you need a decent college to help you get a good job. Look, my friend, you have a lot riding on this little essay in front of you tonight.

Student: That is true.

Devil: As you can see, I am not trying to convince you to do something evil. I am trying to help you out. Give in to temptation now, or spend the rest of the evening distracted. I should be up front with you. I am not going to leave you alone until you give me what I want.

Student: What do you want?

Devil: I want you to be reasonable. I ask for a pittance. Give me what I ask for and I will give you your evening back.

Student: And if I do not?

Devil: I am going to keep pestering you to be reasonable all night. I am in your head. You cannot escape me. You cannot go into another room.

Student: That is true. You and I are actually the same person. I am in your head. You don't see anyone else here, do you? Give me what I want and you will be helping yourself out. This is not wickedness. You know what wicked people do. They kill. They destroy. They ruin. This is between you and me, and I am you. This is practically a victimless crime.

The lesser of two evils is no evil at all, for it preserves a man from greater sin. We must use wisdom and prudence to discern which sin is lesser, after all, and so any course of action arrived at by way of such virtues must be at least a little virtuous, no? However, such delusions may effectively stuff conscience in a closet for an hour while we try to get away with murder, though once we have given in to temptation, it is we ourselves who set conscience free once again. The mature man is the one who realizes before others his age that sin is not worth it.

If death is a practical problem, so is temptation. The work of the Devil is distraction, and he comes to pester us until we give him what he wants. Ancient Christians did not doubt that pagan gods like Jupiter and Zeus existed, though they did not believe pagan gods had positive powers, like sending rain and bringing fertility. However, most Christians did not question the idea that the gods could destroy and torture, as we see in the story of Satan afflicting Job. While rain was the gift of the true God, a demon could only bring bone spurs or boils. If a sick man offered a pagan god some sacrifice for healing, the pagan god might leave the sick man alone and thus it appeared the god had the power to heal. In fact, he merely had the power to harm, but was also at liberty to refrain from harming when he chose. In like manner, temptation nags us and promises to leave us alone if we will offer it a scrap, a tithe. Thus, vicious men who give in to lust and pride in ostentatious ways seem to live enviable lives because we think them least beset by the nagging voices of temptation.

Like Abraham bargaining with Yahweh for the city of Sodom, the Devil is often willing to work and whittle us down to a pittance. However, having done so, he then slowly ratchets his offer back up to something we could not have agreed to in the beginning. Consider, for a moment, a married man at his company's Christmas party. Let us say there is a woman at this party who is beautiful, admirable, and whom the married man thinks of quite highly. The Devil often opens with an outrageous offer, then carefully retreats. As the married man stands conversing with two friends, the woman he admires joins the group to talk.

Devil: She likes you. You should sleep with her.

Man: Obviously not. I would never betray my wife.

Devil: That's not what I said. You don't have to sleep with her. You could kiss her, though. You could tell her you need to discuss something with her privately, something pertaining to work, and then you could kiss her on the mouth when no one was looking. Then you could say, "I'm sorry," in a charming sort of way which would let her know that you like her enough to take her to bed, but that you have other obligations. There would be a tragic sweetness to it. From then on, every time you saw her, you would have that memory of a kiss and you could both savor the fact that sex is desirable, but not feasible. It might even be better than having an actual affair, because those things always wind down in such a tawdry, depressing manner. So don't sleep with her. But kiss her. Passionately. That would not be cheating on your wife. That's not infidelity.

Man: I'm not going to kiss her. My wife would kill me if she found out. I would be heartbroken if I found out my wife had kissed another man, especially if it was some passionate kiss full of longing.

Devil: Don't kiss her, then. That's fine. You still admire her, though. You can let her know how much you admire her. You could embrace her at the end of the evening. It could be the kind of embrace which comes with plausible deniability. The kind of thing which, if your wife saw it, would merely make her think, "If he does anything else with her I'm going to worry, although a simple embrace doesn't warrant too much concern." You could whisper something to her when you hold her, some kind of praise which could be romantic, but might also be professional praise. You could say, "You're amazing." It might mean, "You're an amazing litigator," or it might mean, "You're an amazing woman with amazing legs who looks amazing in that skirt." Who could say? You would know what it meant—if you even wanted it to mean that.

Man: People would notice that kind of thing. It would not look as innocent as you think it would. It has been nine years since I embraced an attractive woman my age who was not my wife, and it left me dazed and nervous.

Devil: Of course. Of course. Don't hold her, don't embrace her. A lot can be communicated through a simple glance, though. A woman can discern the different ways in which a man looks at her. When she speaks, look her in the eyes, and when she stops speaking, keep gazing into her eyes. Have you ever noticed how difficult it is to look someone in the eyes? If you meet someone's gaze and hold it for even a fraction of a second too long, they know. If you want this woman to know what you think of her, you could communicate all of that in the way you look at her. No one would possibly notice. Such a gesture barely even exists.

Man: True. And I have looked at her before, though not what you're describing. Obviously, this sort of thing is not infidelity. Still, this is a Christmas party. I feel bad doing this kind of thing at a Christmas party, especially after my wife told me to have a good time and not hurry back. I am here with the blessing of my wife, and to betray that allowance would make me feel awful. Besides, a glance is not going to be enough to show her how much I admire her.

Devil: She will say something comical in a moment, and when everyone laughs, touch her arm in a familiar way. Have you not seen your wife do the same thing when your friend Joseph tells a joke?

Man: I have.

Devil: It's just a friendly gesture. It means nothing. Look, when we're talking about something as basic as touching someone's arm affectionately, we've left behind every untoward thing we've been talking about for the last several minutes. Touching someone's arm is nothing. A straight man sometimes touches another straight man on the arm when he says something funny. It's nothing.

Man: You're right. I am going to do it.

At this moment, the woman says something comical and the happily married man touches her arm affectionately as everyone laughs at the joke.

Devil: Oh, now you've done it, my friend.

Man: Done what?

At which point the Devil points out how far the happily married man has just gone, and that he has gone further than he thought or intended and that a little more could not possibly do more damage than has already been done.

One of the Devil's greatest triumphs in recent memory was the Satanic Panic of the 1980s, wherein American Christians feared heavy metal, Halloween, Dungeons & Dragons, and even the most banal references to magic. The Devil was reduced to a cartoon, a poorly-disguised clown in red who could be spotted a mile off, and when Christians thought of worshipping the Devil, they thought of people dressed in black, performing prostrations and metanias before a statue of Baphomet. Such a caricature of the Devil constitutes a tragic failure to respect one's enemies. One may judge the shape of society today and make a wager on whether the high alerts of the 1980s were effective, or lulled us into a false state of security.

By contrast, John Milton's Satan is a great student of humanity. Over the course of *Paradise Lost*, Satan is shown to be a master strategist, someone who has been patiently studying man since the Garden, and keeping meticulous notes. Milton's Satan has an overstuffed file on you, and like some world-class football coach, he shows his players videos of your past performances, your wins and losses, and he regularly pauses the tape to make observations on your form. Milton's Satan runs a tight ship, never misses a chance to exploit the fragility of his opponent, and has spent the last several thousand years developing sophisticated tactics to get what he wants. Milton's Satan is willing to adapt to changing circumstances, meets with his field agents on a daily basis to hear progress reports, and never stops honing his craft.

American Christians, on the other hand, give their teenage sons smart phones and say, "Be good."

"But the greatest cause of my sadness is really this—the fact that
in spite of a good helmsman to guide the world, evil can still exist
and even pass unpunished."
- Boethius, 4.1 (p. 85)

"...only the wise can achieve their desire, while the wicked busy
themselves with what gives pleasure without being able to achieve
their real objective. Their actions depend on the belief that they are
going to obtain the good they desire through the things that give
them pleasure. But they do not obtain it, because evil things cannot
reach happiness."
- Lady Philosophy, 4.2 (p. 92)

While the first three books of *The Consolation* are concerned with
the ways a man personally addresses his own temptations to evil
and earthly-mindedness, Book 4 considers the evil in other men's hearts.
Boethius's opening statement echoes the frustration of the Psalmist and
Solomon over the success of the wicked and the failure of the righteous
to thrive. In our own day, skeptics and cynics are apt to prey on Christians in the wake of great tragedies, like tsunamis and school shootings
and earthquakes, as though such terrible events did not also prompt
Christians to wonder about God.

Lady Philosophy promises Boethius that the wicked are always being
punished, and that the righteous are always being rewarded, although
she admits proving this will take some time. Boethius takes the Lady at
her word, but begs her to be quick with an explanation. She begins by
claiming that good men are powerful and evil men weak, for evil men

are incapable of getting what they want, while good men are always moving closer to the fulfillment of their desires. The Lady is here depending on the idea that all men are constantly acting according to what they think best; the will of man is free, and no man uses his autonomy to annoy, confound, or destroy himself. No man acts and claims to himself, in acting, "This will make everything worse."

Temptation invariably presents itself as an asset, an advantage over a more irritating alternative. Sin makes untenable situations tenable, viable, livable, whereas the unsinned alternative is simply too exasperating, too painful, too dangerous to be willfully chosen. If you were to ask a wicked man if he would like to be frustrated and angry, he would deny it, and then continue to act wickedly under the delusion wickedness would alleviate his frustration.

However, wicked men do not achieve the satisfaction they desire, and thus they are continually frustrated by their sin. Why? Sin is pleasurable, but never satisfying. Pleasure is experienced in the body, but satisfaction takes place in the soul, for satisfaction is a cessation of want.

Satisfaction must involve the harmony of intellect, emotion, and appetite—the brain using the heart to control the stomach, as Lewis describes in *The Abolition of Man*. However, in the moment of sin, the soul turns away from God and becomes dark. In sin, the body experiences pleasure, but the soul is rendered incapable of receiving that pleasure and taking enjoyment and satisfaction in it. The disconnect between body and soul in sin might be likened to giving a foot rub to a woman who has just received an epidural. The body is manipulated, but to no end. The effects of anesthetic are even similar to death, for when a man is under anesthetic, his body can be torn apart, and yet he suffers no pain, like a corpse. Sin is an anesthetic of the soul which prohibits satisfaction.

What is true of vice is not true of pleasure, though. The Lady has previously taught that "No man is rich who shakes and groans / Convinced he needs more" (p. 26), a pithy assessment of how vicious desires devour vicious pleasures. However, if a man shakes and groans convinced he needs more faith, he has it. At the point a man is desperate for power, no amount of power will suffice, but if a man is desperate for hope, he will always have enough. Our virtue is exactly proportionate to our desire for it. The desire for hope is hope itself, for obviously a man cannot hope for hope without having it.

The modern Christian is skeptical of this claim, though, for he has confused knowledge and desire. We know that God is good, but we do not much care. After eight hours of work and two hours of errands, I am ready for a drink, a meal, a show. I am aware of God, but I want things. Merely acknowledging that the Resurrection is an historical occurrence is simple, but loving God is difficult.

The damage which evil causes a man is so severe, the Lady suggests the wicked "cease to exist" (p. 91). In the same way we qualify the existence of a dead man, so we should qualify the existence of the wicked. If someone asked, "Is Dante a man?" I could not say, "Yes," but would have to say, "Dante was a man. Now, Dante is a dead man." Were the Lady to encounter a serial pedophile, she would not say, "This is a man," but, "This has the appearance of a living man." While dramatic, these claims should not be read as hyperbole, for the Lady has already established that Goodness and Existence are one, and rejecting the former entails rejection of the latter.

In order to illustrate the powerlessness of vice, I often unfold an elaborate scenario for my students in which I ask them to ruminate on someone their own age getting away not with great evil, but with great mediocrity, while in the presence of profound love.

Imagine, I say, that it is Christmas morning, and that you have not committed any grievous sin for an entire week. You are not on the verge of being discovered. Your sin is behind you and if you would like to make a clean start of it, the possibility of a good and pious life is yours for the taking. And what is more, the idea of being good even seems attractive. Perhaps the sun of righteousness has finally dawned in your heart.

You wake to the smell of coffee, cinnamon, maple, and sage. As you come down the stairs, your mother greets you warmly, embraces you, and gives you a mug of coffee. Your house is warm, and there is a golden, halcyon light filtering through the trees outside the windows. You repeat the word "bliss" to yourself silently several times for no apparent reason, as though that one word might be a complete thought, a prayer, a petition, a creed, and a hope all at once. Passages of Scripture effortlessly appear in your mind, and you think of some claim made about the Messiah turning the hearts of fathers to their children. You do not always see eye to eye with your father, but on this Christmas morning, your father seems nearly like your brother, your friend, a guide whom you trust. He asks you to come over to the window, where you both behold a cloth of white snow covering the earth. All things seem signs and symbols that something good is coming, and perhaps has already arrived.

Your brothers and sisters wake and you wish them a merry Christmas, then you sit beside your tree. Your father and mother have poured a little liquor into their coffee, and soon their cheeks will be flushed pink and your mother will laugh good naturedly at everything. For the first time in your life, you hear your father suggest prayer before opening the gifts and prayer does not seem like a stupid thing adults awkwardly do and require children to do. Rather, prayer seems a natural, fitting, poetic response to the light, the fragrance, the day, the hour. How could we not pray? you wonder. You feel God rarely hears your prayers, for you always mutter them disinterestedly, and yet on this particular Christmas day, you pray with your whole soul and you are confident that Jesus Christ has heard you with delight. In this moment, you are quite grateful to God that you did not smoke marijuana with your friend Daryl two days ago. You often smoke weed with Daryl, but this time you did not, and if you had smoked marijuana with Daryl two days ago, you would be spending this Christmas day wondering if Daryl's mother had found out and, if she had, whether Daryl's mother had texted your mother to tell her. You might be spending this day in a mild state of worry, but no, you smoked no weed and so you have no fears of getting caught. It is more than a month since you smoked week with Daryl, and, for a teen-ager, a month is like ten thousand years and thus beyond the statute of limitations. You are good. God is good. Christmas is good.

By sheer luck, you spent more than you typically do on Christmas presents for your mother and father. For father, a leather-bound journal. For mother, a French press. They are quite pleased with their gifts and comment on how mature you've become, what with your new job bag-ging groceries at Kroger which enables you to buy such adult gifts. Your parents have purchased you a record player and a set of paints and an original pressing of Brian Eno's *The Pearl*, which you had only casually mentioned wanting months ago.

After gifts are opened, your parents have finished their coffee and Benedictine and now your mother is making mimosas and she asks if you would like one, as well. You cannot believe your luck, for your par-ents only let you drink on the rarest of occasions. Drinking on a nearly empty stomach, you are soon savoring a warm, starry euphoria while Handel's *Messiah* begins on the high-fidelity. While you typically find classical music uninteresting, the lofty and courtly air of the day be-fits some bright, Apollonian testimony of God's magnificence, and only something with so many notes and such a choir could possibly suffice. For breakfast, you eat sausage, biscuits, croissants, bacon, quiche aux champignons, raspberries, brioche, crepes, canary melon, and your fa-ther mixes you a Kir Royal to go with your coffee, your grapefruit juice, and your Perrier. Every bite, every morsel, every drop is a revelation, an epiphany of flavor, an oracle of taste. As you eat, you talk, and you find your powers of speech elevated. You are suddenly capable of describing what you have learned over the course of the year. You discourse on philosophy, politics, world events, aesthetics, and all your opinions are received with intrigue and respect, then politely returned with affirma-tive marks that lift you up without flattering or indulging you.

When breakfast is finished the dishes are quickly rinsed, dried, and your father takes you outside where you smoke little cigars and split firewood. Inside, your mother has begun preparing beef tenderloin, broiled Maine lobster, and *pommes presses* for lunch. Your father informs you that your Aunt Sylvia and Uncle Henry will be over in the afternoon for dinner, and your four cousins will be along, too. You have not seen your cousins in three years, and while you often find a full house no small vexation, today you say aloud, "The more the merrier," and, by God, you really mean it.

Around two in the afternoon, there is a knock at the door and your Aunt and Uncle enter, stamping the snow from their feet and happily calling out, "A merry Christmas! A merry Christmas!" Your Aunt greets your mother, your father, and as she moves further into your house, your cousins begin happily stamping in. They are all around your age, fourteen or fifteen or sixteen or so, perhaps a little older, and they greet you with genuine enthusiasm, for, it seems, the idylls of Christmas have settled into their hearts, as well.

However, the last of your cousins to enter is Trent, who is about your age, and who seemed quite different when you saw him last. Upon recognizing him, you realize that he is not dressed in white or red or green as everyone else is, but gray, and his hair is a mess. He carries a backpack and a sullen expression, greets you with a single syllable and then asks, "Where's your TV?"

In the den, which is two rooms away from the kitchen, Trent pulls a game console from his backpack, deftly connects it to your television, sits on the floor several feet away, and begins playing a game wherein he commands a samurai around Manhattan who, from time to time, cuts off the arms of a prostitute who collapses on the concrete, twitches a moment, shrieks, then dies. Every time Trent kills a prostitute, he earns a few points. You are amazed at the rapidity with which Trent went from the door to the game. Your cousin Nancy is still taking off her boots and Trent has already slaughtered five hookers.

The divine trance of the day is broken. In the kitchen, your uncle is laughing while your father tells a story, more coffee is brewing. A dish of fudge, macarons, and raspberry galettes is passed around and your mother is skinning the wax from a bottle of Frangelico. Someone has put on the soundtrack to *A Charlie Brown Christmas* and, somehow, a Cavalier King Charles puppy named Muppet is being giddily passed from one person to the next.

"Did someone get a dog for Christmas?" you ask, looking over your shoulder.

"I got the chainsaw," says Trent absently.

On the screen, Trent's avatar is standing over a woman in a miniskirt and ploughing a small chainsaw through her abdomen. A little dazed, you leave the room and return to the kitchen. For the next hour, you try to leave all thoughts of Trent behind. You seem to be the only one who has noticed him at all, for everyone else in the house is carrying on as though nothing were wrong. In the quiet between one song and the next, the sound of a scream or an explosion faintly issues from the den, but no one seems to notice and you wonder if you are the only one who can hear it.

After a while, you wander back into the den and say, "We're all in the other room being human and eating and drinking and laughing. Do you want to join us, perhaps?"

Trent says, "No, I'm good."

Trent fires a bazooka into a day care.

"Do you really think this kind of game is appropriate for Christmas?" you ask.

"My father got me this game for Christmas," sighs Trent without taking his eyes from the screen.

Shocked, you ask, "Did he know what it was?"

"Yes," says Trent incredulously.

You leave. Trent is a horrible person who cannot be helped, you decide. It would have been better had he never been born. This seems like a harsh judgment to lay against one so young, and yet you are fairly sure that the Lord Himself said it of Judas.

An hour later, Trent's father pokes his head in the den and says, "Time for dinner, Trent."

"Ugh," says Trent, who pauses the game and disgustedly drops the controller on the floor.

Trent stomps his feet into the dining room, where your mother and your aunt have spent an hour laying out your best china, napkins wearing silver rings, three kinds of forks, a massive dish of oysters, candles, wine glasses, water glasses, port glasses, a cutting board loaded with Taleggio, Manchego, and Emmentaler. Trent flops down on the chair beside his place card and looks anxious for everyone to take their seats. While your father comments on the year, on God, on gratitude, Trent alternately looks scared and bored. Within moments of the prayer for the food, Trent has reached across several people's laps to grab from dishes with his fingers, which he then unceremoniously devours in several unchewed bites. He chokes a little on the potatoes, and he seems to do so to prove just how tedious he finds any activity which does not involve eviscerating the innocent. Before the charges and platters have been passed half-way around the table, Trent is finished eating and says, "Can I go?"

On the one hand, you hope the ingratitude, callousness, and disrespect which Trent has shown your family does not go unpunished. On the other hand, Trent is a horrible boor and you really do not want him around, spoiling your dinner with his sighing and his stupid looks.

"You don't want any of the cheese? I thought you enj—" begins your uncle.

"I'm fine. Can I go, please?" asks Trent.

Your Aunt smiles at him and says, "Of course, dear. You go play your game, if you like."

Trent stands from the table, exits the room, and a moment later your cousin Genevieve says the wine tastes like blackberries and smoke and everyone is eagerly tucking into their glasses to see if she is right. Within ten minutes, the laughter has resumed, the stories, the love, the complete self-forgetfulness which a man can know and enjoy only when he is listening to the most engrossing of stories. You forget all about Trent, and Trent forgets all about you and really gives himself over completely to fantasies of murder and rape, for, when no one is looking, he unlocks a code which allows him to undress the hookers in the game and force them to do all sorts of things. Trent is only too happy about the laughing in the next room, for it means everyone is occupied, busy, and thus no one will come in and find him vicariously venting his utter contempt and hatred of the world on some digital woman who has been programmed to whimper, "No. Please, no."

Later, you recall a sermon wherein the pastor said C.S. Lewis believed Hell was "locked from the inside." When you first heard the idea explained you found it insensible, for does Scripture not obviously describe the damned being sent to Hell? Besides, who in their right mind would choose to go to Hell?

However, as you think about the manner in which Trent passed Christmas Day, you cannot think of anything more hellacious than pretending to butcher women and children while your loved ones dine, drink, dance, pray, and embrace one another in the next room over. "The den," you think, "was locked from the inside," for Trent might have left his game whenever he chose.

No one forced him to play, and no one coerced him into wolfing down his food like an animal. For a moment, you imagine the circumstance differently. You imagine that Trent had been locked in a cage in the den, and that he shook the bars of the cage and cried miserably, "Let me out! Please, let me out!" Would his life be better or worse if he were forcibly locked away?

After ruminating on the matter awhile, you decide Trent would be more miserable in a cage of his own making, reveling in pretend mayhem, than if he were put in some strange cage away from his tools of self-destruction. If he wanted out, it would mean he knew what was right. It would mean he knew what Truth and Beauty and Goodness were, even just a little, and that he was justifiably sad to be locked up like a beast. And if Trent had a choice between amusing himself with feigned slaughter or shaking the bars of a cage in protest, would it not be worse to forgo protest and blithely accept villainy?

When I step away from the story, my students can accept the idea that sin is not an ability, but an inability, for speaking of Trent's "power" to play his game all Christmas Day seems absurd. Speaking of Trent's power to walk away from the dinner table is similarly daft. Sin invariably rejects God, brother, sister, mother, father, country, friends, lovers, and creates an insular world wherein the will may seek out whatever end it chooses, unrestrained, unrestricted. Hell is not a place where everyone is finally caught. Hell is a place where men get away with everything. A man's appetite for liquor, drugs, pornography, and television is mitigated in this life by the good people around him who might catch him destroying himself. But in Hell, there are no good people to catch him. There is no one in Hell who is good enough to tell a man, "Stop." If a man has ever avoided the people who love him that he might get away with his sin, he is already in Hell.

With every gratification of sinful desire, the appetite for sin increases. In Hell, men believe they are always increasing their ability to gratify their lusts, when they are merely expanding their lusts. The expansion of lusts is some kind of movement, some kind of alteration, and this movement and alteration is misinterpreted as power. And yet, Lady Philosophy wagers that nothing vexes a man quite like getting the evil things he wants. The wicked man comes to hate the evil things he wants, for they always let him down and never satisfy him, although his longing for them never abates, either.

"It is clear that good deeds never lack reward, or crimes their appropriate punishment. The proper way of looking at it is to regard the goal of every action as its reward, just as the prize for running in the stadium is the wreath of laurels for which the race is run… just as goodness is its own reward, so the punishment of the wicked is their very wickedness."
- Lady Philosophy, 4.3 (p. 93-94)

The Lady is willing to accept that some judgment awaits men upon death, though she does not speak of it often. Following her discussion of evil as suffering, she moves into the teaching that "the goal of every action [is] its reward, just as the prize for running in the stadium is the wreath of laurels" (p. 93). While our actions are directed at other people, we must resign ourselves to the fact that we become the kind of people who do the things we do. An adulterer is an adulterer whether he gets caught or not. The soul bears the impress of the action, even if the action remains unknown.

In the months after I graduated high school, a girlfriend described for me an odd circumstance into which a friend of a friend had fallen. An eighteen-year old high school senior who was an only child had just lost both of his parents in a car crash. His parents had no will, and so he inherited a house, a car, and all their wealth and possessions. There was no one else he could stay with, for both his parents had been only children as well, so, since the boy was legally an adult, he decided to continue living in his parents' home. My girlfriend said,

"Some people I know are going to this guy's house tonight to watch a movie. Let's go." We went.

When we stepped through the front door, I saw a perfectly unassuming two-story residential home with uninteresting photographs framed on the wall, a coat rack, a dresser near the door upon which sat a little porcelain dish of car keys and loose change. And yet, something about the home felt eerie and unnatural. In the living room, half a dozen teenagers sat smoking, none of whom I recognized, and they were all watching a movie. This was the first time I ever set foot in a family residence—a place which featured the design preferences of a mother—wherein human beings were freely smoking. While I was a smoker at the time, I was nonetheless uncomfortable by the vulgarity of smoking inside the home of a woman who, given her taste for décor, would never have allowed it had she been alive. After watching the movie for half an hour, the barely legal owner of the house left the living room and walked down the halfway to another room, which he entered and then closed the door. A moment passed, I heard a glass bottle break.

The film went on and eventually I asked the group where the bathroom was and someone pointed to the same room into which the owner had gone. With some trepidation, I knocked on the door and entered. The room had formerly been the master bedroom, though it now smelled of urine, beer, and spray paint. Strange messages were scrawled on the walls. Broken bottles and broken wood littered the floor. The windows were covered over with paper or aluminum foil. A more fitting place to torture a man does not readily come to mind. The owner stood still, bewildered, holding a baseball bat.

"I need to use the bathroom," I said, trying to behave as though nothing was out of place. I recall there was an ironing board set up for no apparent reason.

He mumbled ascent and gestured with the bat to an attached bathroom. While I was in the bathroom, which was almost entirely untouched by his madness, he continued laying into the walls and the furniture, which was only a few feet away. In like manner, the rest of the house appeared in fine condition. No other room had been attacked.

When I finish telling this story to students, I often ask, "Did the fellow get away with what he did?" The half of the class which answers first says, "Yes. No one was around to catch him," which is entirely true.

While his parents were alive, they might have grounded him for something as trivial as drawing on the wall or failing to pick up broken glass, but once his parents died, no one was around to punish him, for there is nothing illegal about destroying a room in your own house. A moment later, however, a few students will say, "No. He did not get away with it," although they often become tongue-tied when trying to explain why. Having destroyed the room, he must live with it. His punishment is being the kind of person who destroys the good things his parents left to him. Or his punishment is having a room in his lovely family home ruined. When my students pity the boy, they pity him as someone who no longer fears getting caught.

A man's soul might be likened to a house in which his very being resides. He is free to make his soul as fine a place as he chooses. If a man collects beautiful ideas, those ideas are like books which fill the shelves in the home of the soul. Acts of charity and generosity make the home of the soul spacious, and love makes the windows of the soul tall and orients those windows toward the sunrise. The ordered celebration of fasts and feasts, holidays and ceremonies and rituals of all kinds keep the home of the soul orderly, tidy, swept, dusted. However, the sinful passions of a man scratch up the upholstery, break the windows, overturn the tables, and piss on the carpets, and he gets away with it all, so to speak. Plenty of vices are simple enough to hide from the world, although the more vicious a man becomes, the more dilapidated and infested the home of his soul. The more a man puts himself in the pocket of sin, the less his soul is a companion. The soul-as-companion becomes evermore dumb, evermore deaf as a man gives himself to lust, drunkenness, violence, pride. As pornography, drugs, and abuse become habitual to a man, his visits with the soul-as-companion become more brief, more incoherent and troubling. The companion eventually refuses to allow the man into his own soul, and a man is exiled without, incapable of contemplation, meaning, significance, patience. He sleeps when he is tired, eats when he is hungry. He has become like an animal.

"It may seem incredible to some, but it must be the case that the wicked are less happy if they achieve their desires than if they are unable to do what they want. For, if desiring something wicked brings misery, greater misery is brought by having had the power to do it, without which the unhappy desire would be unfulfilled... the wicked are happier if they suffer punishment than if they are unrestrained by any just retribution."
- Lady Philosophy, 4.4 (p. 96-97)

That the wicked "are happier if they suffer punishment than if they are unrestrained" (p. 97) is obvious to anyone who has tired of the anxiety which attends continually getting away with sin. Few men want to confess their sin, but they dream of how good life might be today had they confessed their sin a year ago. A man wants to be done with his sin, but he does not want to suffer the embarrassment of cutting himself off from it, for truly breaking entrenched sinful habits requires the help of others who then become aware of his struggle. Hence, a man tries to deal with his sin on his own. He tells himself, "I will confess this sin, but I will confess it a year from now. I will not commit this sin for a year. Confessing a sin I committed this morning would be mortifying, but confessing something I have not done in a year will hardly be embarrassing at all. In a year, I will confess I formerly had a problem with a certain sin, and the people to whom I confess this will be impressed that I have done so well on my own. They will see my commitment to goodness. I will look forward to their praise, and this anticipation will make it easy to keep from temptation for a year. In fact, I have already defeated this sin, I simply need to wait a year before I tell anyone I have defeated it." Of course, the man goes right on committing his sin, and he exonerates himself with this tidy little speech from time to time, especially when pride seems an easier way of dealing with his shortcomings than guilt.

The Lady's address of the guilty conscience is so apt, I cannot fail to think the historical Boethius lived much of his life fearful of being found out—for what, I have no idea. As a high school teacher, I am surrounded by human beings who live in a constant fear of being found out. The average student sees five or six different teachers a day, a multitude of rulers, all of whom have varying degrees of interest in enforcing the rules. Some teachers in a classical school care about the dress code, others do not. Some teachers sit gossiping, flirting friends on opposite sides of the classroom, others do not. Some teachers keep a close eye on students taking tests and quizzes, others do not. Some teachers are careful about policing the cruelty of bullies, others do not care at all. Beside all this, an individual teacher is often uneven in his commitment to enforcing the rules. On Monday, his schedule is lean enough to enforce the dress code, but on Tuesday he is too busy to worry about small infractions. Having quickly addressed themselves to the gaps in the system, students are often looking to get away with something. Violations of the dress code are hardly the extent of student rebellion, but a barometer which measures how many less obvious things the students are simultaneously trying to get away with.

Having once been a high school student, and not a very good one at that, I can attest to the deleterious effects which the fear of getting caught has on an ability to pay attention in class. Fear of getting caught hijacks the imagination and destroys a student's ability to suspend his disbelief or give himself over to the logic of a lecture or sermon. On a number of occasions, I have found students willing to sit in cockeyed, uncomfortable positions in their chairs merely to get away with wearing their shirt untucked in class. The young algebra student who fears his mother will greet him in the afternoon with, "So, about the search history on your laptop…" is not going to hear a word his teachers say. While moral instruction is not merely for the moral, the more recently a conscience has been cleaned, the greater the student's capacity to hear instruction in virtue.

To illustrate this point, I sometimes conduct a rather straightforward shakedown, although I do not announce it as such. From time to time, I will open class on a Monday morning with:

> *Have you all been following the rules lately? Perhaps you have not. Perhaps you have recently broken the rules, and you are now in that period where you are wondering if you got away with what you did. I know how it is. You break the rules, and then the waiting begins.*

> *For most of your sins and crimes, if you have not been found out after three days, you are safe. The odds of being discovered more than three days after the fact are slim. But for three days, you are on edge. Perhaps you are in that waiting period right now. When your mother picks you up from school, you try to feel her out. Has she discovered anything over the course of the day? Has a teacher called? Has the principal? You ask your mother a few polite questions, and if she responds politely, she knows nothing. If your mother knows, the very air in the car will be charged with her displeasure and you will feel it the moment you get in. Your mother's unhappy mouth, the searching look in her eyes, slight differences in the way she turns her neck to regard you when you speak.*

> *At other times, your mother is hard to read. You get in the car after school and she is unhappy, but also tired, and perhaps she is not angry with you, just with her life and the whole world. You hope this is the case. You would rather your mother was miserable than that she discovered what you said or what you smoked. When you are uncertain if you have been found out, you become very kind. You ask your*

mother, "Are you okay? Is anything wrong? Can I do anything for you?" You hope she says, "Just a little tired." That is fine. That is a good answer.

However, your mother is not the whole story. There is also your father, who may know. Perhaps you have done something significant enough that a teacher phoned your father directly. Perhaps you have done something so bad, your father has decided not to tell your mother just yet. When your father gets home from work, you gauge him, just as you did with your mother. He is easier to read than your mother. You can tell within moments of his return home whether he knows anything.

Of course, none of this has to do with this moment, in this class, right now, and the possibility that I know about something you've done. So let me make you this offer: If you come and confess to me what you've done before lunch, I will go very easy on you. If not, the situation will change and things will become much more complicated.

I know what you are thinking. There are twenty students in this class. You are personally aware of many things which other students are currently hoping to get away with. If I actually know what one of you has done—and that hasn't been established, because right now, this whole speech is purely speculative—but if I actually have real knowledge of some bad thing which one of you has done, the odds that it is you seem pretty low. It is far more likely that I have someone else figured out.

However, you are concerned. The Devil has just whispered to you, "He doesn't know. This is a classic shakedown. He's got nothing. This is a horribly crass way of getting a confession." But you know the Devil always overplays his hand. The Devil always tells you that you *won't get caught, but sometimes you do.*

You are intrigued by what I said about getting off easy if you confess before lunch. You wonder, "How easy? A one-day suspension? Three days? Maybe just detention. Maybe just a talking to. I can endure a talking to. I will look contrite and say the humble things about sin and grace. Perhaps it will all take less than twenty minutes. I could still play soccer during lunch, maybe."

You know that I, Joshua Gibbs, am not a very good person, for I have told you so on many occasions. Would it not be easier to confess your sin to someone who admits he is a rotten person? "Perhaps if I confess my sin to Gibbs, he and I can deal with it alone, but if I do not confess it to Gibbs, then other people will have to get involved— and those other people have not admitted they are pretty rotten. Gibbs is into works righteousness. I'm pretty sure he's trying to earn his way to Heaven, and given how rotten he has admitted he is, I suppose he thinks he is going to Hell. Maybe if I confess to him, he will be merciful to me because he thinks it means God will be merciful to him."

At the same time, you're thinking, "Of course, I don't want to confess my sin for nothing. What if I confess and it turns out he didn't know all along? I would be his fool. I would have fallen for it. Now, confessing your sin is the right thing to do, obviously, but I have already confessed the sin in question to God. I have already been forgiven of the thing I did. That means I don't have to confess it to anyone else."

The rest of your morning is shot, though. You know now that you will think of nothing else until lunch passes. Your mind is wandering ahead, though. This instance of "getting away with it" is far more dicey than these things usually get. If you do not confess your sin before lunch, and it turns out the boy in front of you gets nailed for something, you will nonetheless regard it as a close one. In the past, you have completely gotten away it, but if you get away with it this time, you will have narrowly escaped being found out. If you get away with it this time, you will never do it again.

But that's not true. The only thing which keeps you from giving into this sin full bore is the fear of getting caught. If you get away with it this time, you are obviously untouchable. The adults can get close, but no matter how close they get, you still escape unscathed. If you get away with it this time, you never need to fear getting caught again. You will have danced on a razor's edge. If you get away with it this time, you will be more brazen, more audacious in the future. You will have proved to yourself that man cannot touch you, and you know God has more than enough grace to cover a lifetime of revelry, so you're fine on that front, as well.

You know something about shakedowns, though, and you know shakedowns work because most human beings have guilty consciences and weak stomachs. The only way to survive a shakedown is to develop strong nerves. You realize that this kind of shakedown only takes place when there isn't enough evidence to prove anything, so a confession is needed. You think, "Gibbs has not said anyone needs to come forward and confess anything. He has used words like "perhaps" and "maybe." He's covering for the weakness of his position, so that if nothing happens, he can play it off as nothing more than a normal lecture, or a gag. In fact, if no one comes forward, he's screwed. He is desperate for a confession no one offered."

On the other hand, this little speech has quite a few layers at this point. Ten minutes ago, you might not have known that a shakedown is called "a shakedown." I have revealed to you the weakness of shakedowns and the potential weakness of this shakedown, if that is

actually what this is. Strong nerves— I have even given you sugges-
tions on how to beat a shakedown. I have given you plenty of outs,
plenty of reasons to dismiss this as a gag. I do strange things in class
from time to time, and maybe this is one of them. I suppose you will
find out by lunch.

The guilty conscience, the state of mind born of constantly getting away with it, is a miserable Cold War story of mistrust, an epistemological nail-biter wherein the soul descends into a chaos of accusation and self-defense, loneliness and delusion. A man may get away with it, but he never gets away with getting away with it.

CHAPTER FIVE

On Pedagogy

> "I who once wrote songs with joyful zeal
> Am driven by grief to enter weeping mode."
> - Lady Philosophy, 1.1 (p. 3)

T*he Consolation* opens with Boethius caught up in self-pity, for self-pity is the root from which all earthly consolations grow. The song which begins the book is not merely a song of lamentation, for Boethius has invited the muses to come and sing tragic songs to him that he might indulge his grief more deeply. When Lady Philosophy arrives in his cell, she need not know the reason for his weeping, though she quickly judges it decadent and destructive. For our part, Boethius is like a young man who, upon arriving home in the afternoon, morosely and silently casts his school things to the floor and tromps up the stairs to his room, slams the door, then begins playing his loudest, saddest rock and roll records. Whether or not Boethius has been wronged is of little consequence to Lady Philosophy, who knows that she cannot reason with a man in such a frame of mind. She refers to him as "sick," which means she sees the rising darkness in his heart. Boethius is not merely out of sorts, he is mired in sin.

Recognizing that Boethius is in sin is essential to understanding *The Consolation of Philosophy*. He has been wronged, but he is also wronging himself and God. In the course of Book I, we hear Boethius give an account of the horrific injustices he has suffered at the hands of lawless men. Lady Philosophy spends relatively little time consoling Boethius for the pain of these injustices, but is very interested in leading him out of a dark wood. *The Consolation* is intended to console those who have been mistreated by men or crushed by misfortune, but the book is also a series of jarring meditations on the goodness of God which can shake us out of the trance of habitual sin. Lady Philosophy offers Boethius "gentle medicine" for his psychic aches and pains, but she also abruptly turns off his sad music and roundly insults the singers. She does not arrive with her hat in her hand, but with a sharp sword proceeding from her mouth.

The opening chapters of the book must be preached, and the good teacher will treat *The Consolation* as a call to overcome the besetting sin in his own life. Boethius learns to conquer the self-pity which has darkened his understanding, corrupted his memory, and overwhelmed his hope in God. Contemporary readers will bring their own vices to the book, and the teacher should call on students to take stock of their own souls before moving beyond the first chapter.

Having recognized that Boethius is in sin, readers will also note that the muses are demonic, for they are inciting and aggravating their patient to greater depths of self-pity. The demons which beset Boethius in the first chapter of the book are not attacking his mind, but his heart.

In *The Abolition of Man*, C.S. Lewis teaches that every man possesses three separate realms of will; the brain is an icon of what a man knows, the heart is an icon of what he loves, and the stomach is an icon of what he wants, or his appetite for pleasant things. All three of these wills must be properly ordered and work in harmony with one another in order for a man to live a free and virtuous life. The stomach is more powerful than the brain, though, and the brain must have the aid of the heart in order to govern the stomach. In other words, it is not sufficient for a man to know what is right, he must love what is right. If a man does not love what is right, his stomach will bully his mind. He may know getting drunk is sin, but such knowing will not keep him sober if he has a strong appetite for liquor. Rather, he must also love the virtue of temperance and the only way to do this is to love temperate men. He must be surrounded by men who will love him for his temperance. If the heart does not work in concert with the mind, a man will lay down for temptation like an obedient dog.

Of course, such ideas about brain, heart, and stomach assume the heart can be governed and that mere knowledge is insufficient for virtue. Both of these beliefs are odious to modern men. Living in a society which is downstream from the Enlightenment, we tend to think knowing is sufficient. Knowing is easier than doing, and many modern Christians are positively terrified of the idea that doing anything is truly necessary, for we are "saved by faith and not by works." On the other hand, we also live downstream from the Romantics, and modern men bristle at the idea that the heart can and should be taught. We prefer to see the heart as both the essence of a man and something set apart from a man. Inasmuch as the heart is set apart from a man, he cannot be held accountable for the arbitrary feelings into which his heart plunges him, hence the typically modern claim, "I wish I loved you, but I just don't feel that way," or, "I just cannot help loving you." However, inasmuch as the heart is the essence of a man, moderns believe that any attempt to govern or corral the heart is tyrannical and thuggish. Accordingly, we hold that a man may love whatever he wants, whoever he wants, however he wants, to whatever degree he wants, and anyone who says otherwise is inhuman.

As an educated philosopher, Boethius has a well-trained mind, and so when we find him crying in his cell, the problem is not ignorance, but that he has forgotten Wisdom, his first love. His heart has strayed. For this cause, Lady Philosophy calls the muses playing up his sadness "hysterical sluts" (p. 4), implying Boethius has been unfaithful to her.

While she will soon become the consoling mother, Philosophy enters the scene as a spurned lover.

While students encountering *The Consolation* for the first time will doubtless meet new ideas, the book ultimately proves to be about loving what is good, not merely knowing what is true. The most successful battles I have waged with temptation have taken place in my heart, not in my mind. It is only on rare occasions that I am genuinely confused about what doing the right thing entails. However, I regularly do not want to do what is right.

Early in my marriage I came to realize that Scripture was no talisman for warding off sin; I regularly give in to temptation while passages of Scripture condemning the very thing I am doing pass through my head. On the other hand, when I was tempted to the degradations of lust, I typically found that imagining my wife's face distorted by tears was such a talisman. Any man battling the temptation to lust will do far better changing his computer desktop to an image of his wife rather than some artist's representation of stone tablets containing the Ten Commandments. This is not necessarily because a man loves his wife more than God (though most men do, in my experience), but because a wife is the living embodiment of the seventh commandment; a spouse is the incarnation of an abstract moral precept.

Between the brain, the heart, and the stomach, the heart is the organ which requires the most training. Most men do not need to be taught that stealing is wrong, and most men do not need to be taught to want food and sex and clothing. But the heart is another matter. Teaching a man to love what is right takes some doing, for right things are rarely pleasant in and of themselves. Even after the muses have been sent away, Lady Philosophy still has much work to do in order to turn Boethius's heart back to God.

The good teacher knows there is little point in appealing only to a student's mind, because between the mind, the heart, and the stomach, the mind is inherently weakest. I do things I know are wrong all the time, but I rarely do things which are physically unpleasant. I often say, "I really need to jog more," and I rarely say, "I really need to drink more imperial stouts," because drinking imperial stouts is pleasant and so I do it all the time, while jogging is a genuine hassle. The good teacher is not satisfied by appeals to the mind, but presses on for the heart, as well, knowing the mind and heart can together overrule the stomach and bring a man's appetites under control. The teacher who underestimates his task, believing he must appeal only to the intellect, is a milquetoast and a bore. He sits to lecture, speaks in a calm voice, employs modest hand gestures, and is never carried away by his own stories or the stories of others. His own heart is not on the line, and so neither are the hearts of his students. He offers his students his brain, and his students will offer their brains in return, but great minds fail when they are not married to great hearts.

> **"It is hardly surprising if we are driven by the blasts of storms when our chief aim on this great sea of life is to displease wicked men."**
> **-Lady Philosophy, 1.3 (p. 8)**

While Boethius has given in to sinful self-pity, we learn in his short autobiography in 1.4 that he has been incarcerated unjustly. What opens up to the reader, then, is two divergent conversations: how a man responds to suffering he imposes on himself, by which I mean a man's own sin, and how he responds to suffering unfairly imposed on him from without, by which I mean the sin of others. Inasmuch as Boethius suffers innocently at the hands of others, he assumes the figure of Job. Both Job and Boethius are led into suffering because they are righteous, for it is the piety of Job which arouses Satan's ire against him; had Job lived a life of spiritual mediocrity, he might have avoided Satan's notice.

Americans often speak quite casually of "drawing close to God," as though it were a labor to take up lightly over the weekend, but the lives of great men like Job or the Apostles testify to the danger of living near God. I once had a friend whose sexual sin had lately been discovered by his wife, and his marriage was thus on the verge of dissolving. He undertook a forty-day fast, though I did not know he had begun the fast until he was several weeks into it. A large group of friends went out to dinner, but he ordered orange juice. In speaking with him, and in hearing how much of his life he had devoted to prayer since the beginning of his fast, it was obvious that he had drawn very close to God. He was quiet, calm, contemplative, capable of lucidly examining his own soul and returning honest, heartbreaking judgements. He was nonetheless hopeful, newly intrigued by life, humbled by his failures, grateful for the ineffable mercy of a second chance to live anew. On the other hand, he looked like a wreck. The healthy weight of his body had begun falling from his frame and his eyes had sunk back into his head. Drawing close to God is a work which is usually attended by heavy costs. While God is always willing to listen, we are rarely willing to truly speak to Him, but my friend had undertaken the harrowing task of laying his body and soul bare so that he could talk with God undistracted, focused, and say what he really meant. Boethius has been given time and space to draw close to God before he dies, though he is intimidated by the thought of letting go of his claim to righteousness and all the good things which came with that righteousness. Boethius is like Job in that he is suffering for his righteous deeds, but unlike Job in his complaints. Job never complained of the loss of his worldly goods. He only demanded to speak with God. His friends tempted him to confess his sin that he might be forgiven, make sacrifices, and get his wealth back, but Job had no sin to confess and neither was he interested in the restoration of his earthly kingdom. Boethius is not exactly in the same circumstance as Job; however, when *The Consolation* begins, he believes he is. Lady Philosophy must first show Boethius that he is no Job.

Lady Philosophy speaks of the righteous displeasing "wicked men," which might, at first blush, not seem to have much to do with the life of a high school student. However, the hallways of Christian schools are nevertheless daily beset by the petty evils of adolescence: willing violations of the dress code, gossip, vulgar jokes, aimless complaining, crass language, laziness, and lies. While these kinds of sins are par for the teenage course, I often find myself preaching to those students who watch their fellows commit these sins and offer no resistance, no rebuke, no aid to teachers who have to pick up the pieces.

Once, when teaching an Old Testament history class, I asked a class of seventh-grade boys to write a sermon to their classmates using an event from the life of David as their text. "Tell your classmates what they really need to hear. Tailor the sermon to seventh-grade struggles," I said. Over two-thirds of them wrote sermons about the slaying of Goliath, wherein they exhorted their classmates to take courage and share the Gospel with unbelievers. This was, apparently, the kind of generically pious thing many had learned to responsively say when asked about anything pertaining to the Bible, so they were taken back when I told them God did not need them to share the Gospel with anyone. "By your own report, most of you are bored in church and rarely read your Bibles," I said, "so I don't know why you think you are competent to share the Gospel. Most of you are so disinterested in God that it is like pulling teeth to get you to sing a single hymn in chapel every morning, because you are quietly joking and laughing with the people beside you. You don't really know what the Gospel is, and if you tried to answer difficult questions about the Gospel, I am fairly certain you would get most of the details wrong. No, God does not need you to share the Gospel. What God needs from you is obedience in small rules—the kind of rules you can get away with breaking. God needs you to be willing to be embarrassed in front of your peers, which is the thing you hate the most. God wants you to do what you don't want to do—tell your classmates to put away their phones when they pull them out in the restroom, because that's a violation of school rules. God wants you to confess your secret sins to your parents and get help with problems you can't master on your own, problems which you sink further into every day. And when your classmates mock you as a saint for doing these good things, God needs you to stand there and take it. Telling yourself that your chief spiritual need is to repeat a Gospel that you are bored by and confused by is a way of getting around the more urgent matters of your spiritual health."

Drawing close to God is dangerous, for the righteousness of God will elicit confessions of guilt from men, and God will begin purging the sin from a man's soul. Sin does not come out of a man except by confession, and confession often comes with a heavy price tag. Being purged of sin is both exhilarating and mortifying, which is exactly why most people want to remain a comfortable distance from God, neither so close so as to make a full and honest confession, but neither too far away that feelings of alienation set in.

> **"But you say you are eager to hear more. You would be more than eager if you knew the destination I am trying to bring you to." I asked what it was and she told me that it was true happiness. "Your mind dreams of it," she said, "but your sight is clouded by shadows of happiness and cannot see reality." I begged her to lead on and show me the nature of true happiness without delay.**
> **- *The Consolation*, 3.1 (p. 47)**

Let us imagine a young man named Henry graduates from high school and goes off to college, where he will undertake a five-year degree in architecture. Let us also imagine that Henry promptly joins a fraternity. Fraternal life is much like Henry imagined it would be. After the first full week of classes, Henry returns to the Beta House where he finds one of his brothers has purchased three massive jugs of rot gut whiskey and that everyone has plans to get profoundly, biblically drunk on the stuff and then attend a party at a sorority down the street. Desperate to be loved and approved, Henry drinks a manly portion of liquor and then totters down the street with the rest of the hunters. Saturday evening passes in a similar fashion, the bacchanals are tempered a touch on Sunday, and Monday morning the brothers all pronounce the weekend a rollicking success.

And so Henry passes the first, second, third, and fourth years of life in college. He collects a few girlfriends, a few mild and treatable sexually transmitted diseases, and a few citations for disorderly conduct. During his fifth year, his architecture program is far more demanding, he settles a little, but does not fail to collect a few more notches on his bedpost.

After he graduates, Henry accepts an entry level position at an architecture firm and quickly discovers that the kinds of exploits which won him fame in college have little purchasing power in the world of business. Around the water cooler, no one brags of blondes or body shots, but contracts and projects. Henry soon learns a new language of honor and glory. In his third year with the firm, he marries a coworker. Two years after his marriage, his first child is born. Three years after that, another child. And so Henry slowly becomes an adult, a responsible man, who is twice tempted to have an affair and yet does not. He does not mind the company of his children, and after ten years of marriage, still enjoys an occasional date with his wife.

On his fortieth birthday, he takes his wife out to dinner at a fancy restaurant, orders beef bourguignon, but does not finish it. "You've lost some weight recently," remarks his wife, observing the food left on his plate when the waiter takes away the dish. "Have I?" he asks, and his wife is incredulous. "You haven't even been trying, have you?" she asks, and he shakes his head. After a moment Henry says, "I haven't had much of an appetite lately." Before bed that evening, his wife suggests he see a doctor. "Unexplained weight loss is not good," she says.

Henry goes to his doctor and receives a physical and a cancer screening, neither of which reveal anything troubling. "You're in good health," says his doctor, "so why the weight loss?" Henry shrugs. His doctor asks, "Have you been depressed lately?" After considering the question a moment, Henry says, "I suppose so. A little." His doctor asks why, and Henry says he does not know. His doctor says, "You should see a psychiatrist." Henry is taken aback to hear this, for he has never thought of himself as the kind of person who might need psychiatric help. He tells his physician he will consider it, and after a few days, he makes an appointment, though he does not tell his wife. When Henry meets with the psychiatrist, the first question he is asked is, "Where and when were you happiest?"

For as straightforward and obvious a question as this seems, Henry has never considered it before. He says, "The day I got married, I think." Henry says this out of a sense of duty, the same kind of duty which prompts even the impious to attend church on Christmas and Easter. After saying it, Henry wonders if it is true, though he does not have time enough to consider it during the appointment. That night, he lays awake and thinks it over.

When much younger, Henry spent a season of his life "abandoned to pleasure" (p. 49), as Lady Philosophy says, although the idea of declaring that time to be the happiest of his life seems depressing. On the other hand, Henry wants to say that the day he became a husband or the day he became a father was the happiest day of his life, though he wonders if these answers are social conventions he has learned from romantic films and greeting cards. The day he became a father was fearful, anxious, for his wife was in labor nine hours, and during the last five he was secretly angry she had not opted for a caesarean. Perhaps when the doctor placed his daughter in his arms was a proud moment, a sublime moment, though Henry cannot shake the feeling he must dig deeper.

As a child, when Henry entered the kitchen to see his mother was cooking, she would angrily shush him out. He recalls a certain Christmas when he was eight years old and his paternal grandparents were coming to dinner. They loved him and spoiled him, though his mother was always nervous and clumsy in their presence. In the days before they came, his mother would always snap at him and chide him more than usual; however, on this particular Christmas, his mother was calm, kind, and asked Henry if he would help her prepare dinner in the kitchen. He pulled a chair from the dining room table into the kitchen, stood on it, and his mother let him whip the potatoes with the electric mixer. He helped her for an hour, set the table, and his mother did not fuss the fact he could not get the napkins and forks straight. Laying awake in bed more than three decades later, Henry decides that this day was the happiest of his entire life.

Book 3 of *The Consolation* is about real happiness and fake happiness and it will make little sense to students who are not first asked to spend time dwelling on the happiest days of their own lives. I tell the story about Henry and ask them why Henry would probably not declare his wild college days to be the happiest of his life. Their answers are straight forward, but not shallow. They say Henry would be ashamed to say his happiest days were in college, for it would suggest his marriage and children meant less to him than his own pleasure. When the Lady speaks of happiness, she is not talking of pleasure, but satisfaction and joy and contentment. These are not subjects which the Devil wants us to dwell on, for they always reveal the things he offers as pale forgeries.

Childhood bears a certain likeness to Adam and Eve's unfallen days with God in the Garden of Eden. In adolescence, children become aware of themselves as sexual beings. They know they are naked, so to speak. Like Adam and Eve, they want to hide and they want to dress themselves. Upon seeing the way Adam and Eve have dressed, God says, "You're not leaving the Garden dressed like that." Teenagers have been arguing with their parents about clothes since the beginning. Teenagers are aware of the happiness, innocence, and naiveté which attend childhood. If you ask a room full of high school sophomores, "Have you become more and more righteous with each passing year? Are you closer to God now than you were when you were eight?" very few will answer in the affirmative. When I was first asked this question in high school, my answer was the same answer my students typically give. "No. In fact, with every passing year of my life since I turned seven or eight, I have become more sinful."

When I was a child, I sought the attention and affection of my parents and resisted enticements to lie and steal just because such things were wrong and made me feel guilty. I thought highly of my mother, loved her sincerely, and imagined she would receive a high place in Heaven, next to the throne of God Himself. By the time I was sixteen, however, I was desperate to get away from my parents whenever I could. I do not mean that I was zealous to move out, get an apartment and a job of my own, but that any evening which allowed me to go out with my friends was a good evening. By the time I was eighteen, nearly everything I looked forward to doing had to be done in secret. I loved my parents, but they had largely become obstacles, things to maneuver around in order to get what I wanted. From time to time, I briefly considered the fact that I was not becoming more righteous, and that with every passing year, lies and deception were more common to my speech. A black cloud of fear that I would someday get caught constantly hung about my head. Even at such a young age, I would have said that my happiest days were long ago. Nonetheless, I continued pursuing secret pleasures. The fact that I knew my happiest days were behind me did not make me want to seek them out again.

Of course, absolutely nothing keeps a man from pursuing the profound happiness he claimed as a child. An adult's desires are far more complex than a child's desires, but satisfying these desires rarely makes a man as happy as he was when he only wanted the love of his mother and father. Adults want sex, money, time, liquor, fit and healthy bodies, praise, the admiration of their peers, not to mention clothes and houses and cars that will sufficiently impress their friends. Lady Philosophy asks us whether attaining these things provides real happiness, or merely illusions and "shadows of happiness" (p. 47). I often spend my time and money acquiring things I would be embarrassed to claim gave me real satisfaction.

The real happiness which Lady Philosophy brings into discussion toward the end of Book 3 is not something which any man may experience on earth, for it is full union with God. However, asking a man to identify the happiest day of his life will also reveal the trajectory of life. Is he seeking the things which actually make him happy? Granted, an adult has responsibilities far beyond those of a child, and so gainful employment eventually becomes a necessity; however, the fact that adults have greater responsibilities than children by no means suggests adults must seek happiness through radically different means than children. If a man realizes that, at his happiest, he is merely performing some benign task in the company of people he loves, that man is by no means obligated to continue pursuing the pleasures of sex, money, time, liquor. The only thing which holds a man back from pursuing genuine happiness is his lack of desire to do so.

The happiest day of my own life occurred just two years ago, on an evening I took my family out to dinner. We had plans to eat and then attend a choral performance by the students at the school where I teach. The restaurant was nothing particularly fancy, just a straight forward American menu, although my seven-year-old daughter Camilla was unusually grateful to go out for dinner. She saw root beer on the menu, then asked if she could order one. I told her she could, and she excitedly asked my wife, "Did you like root beer when you were a kid?" Paula said she did. When the root beer arrived, Camilla poured it from the bottle into a glass, tasted it, pronounced it good with deathless enthusiasm, then insisted her mother taste it. Paula tasted it, declared it very good, and then Camilla said, "Do you like root beer? We both like root beer! We're twins. Dad, take a picture of me and mommy next to this root beer!" I obliged. I commented to my wife that I had never seen the child happier in all her life, and for something as trivial as a soft drink. She sustained this level of joy for nearly an hour. Later, I looked at the photo

I took and found it a profound icon of innocent joy.

That God should allow me to take a photograph which so perfectly represents the child's happiness is both a gift and a burden. This picture is never far from me. I see it several times a day. If I gaze at it for more than a moment, involuntary tears fill my eyes. I want this image impressed as deeply in my consciousness as possible. I want the image to come back to me in moments of temptation, and I want the goodness of the image itself to cut through the delusions of fake happiness which the Devil inevitably brings. Once a man has participated in the real joy of a child, he knows why he is alive. He knows his purpose. When I give in to temptation, I reject the image of true happiness. When I sin, I wish away my daughter's happiness, unmake it, steal it. Fake happiness is not second-best to real happiness. Fake happiness is at war with real happiness.

Lady Philosophy's comments about "real happiness" will be of little value if they are not firmly attached to an authentic relic of real happiness in the reader's mind. While the Lady is leading Boethius to contemplate the happiness which comes with full and final union with God, the beatific vision spills backwards over time and in moments of selflessness we receive foretastes here and now. Such moments are not simply brief, pleasant respites from the difficulties of being finite and mortal. Rather, such moments are inspired and sacred texts God writes on our hearts. The man who has no vision of real happiness, who has not contemplated the difficulties and rarities of real happiness, will not be capable of learning and practicing virtue.

Teachers commonly fail to connect their subject to real happiness, real satisfaction, and real thriving, but reduce the need to know the Romantics, or algebra, or geography to the possibility of a certain line of work in the future. A colorful poster on the wall of the math room catalogs all the jobs which require a knowledge of mathematics, and, lo and behold, there are many. Curiously absent from such lists are drug dealer, pimp, prostitute, bank robber, gambler, and panhandler, all jobs in which mathematics are just as helpful as for the architect, accountant, and meteorologist. Even the fellow who is paid in cigarettes to let the other inmates know when the guards are coming would do best to know a thing or two about distance and foot speed. Of course, we do not want to think of our children using mathematics in such awful employments, but if we do not teach virtue, we are merely raising crafty villains. Was it mercy or history which Stalin failed to learn in high school? If school lessons do not regularly return to contemplations of real happiness, the teacher is either actively teaching false happiness or blithely allowing students to pursue misery while he disinterestedly watches.

> **Then I spoke to her and said that she was well aware of
> how little I had been governed by worldly ambition. I had
> sought the means of engaging in politics so that virtue
> should not grow old unpraised. "And that," she replied
> "is the one thing that could entice minds endowed with
> natural excellence though not yet perfected with the fin-
> ishing touch of complete virtue—the desire for glory, the
> thought of being famed for the noblest of services to the
> state. But just think how puny and insubstantial such
> fame really is.'"**
> *- The Consolation,* 2.7 (p. 40)

I f the good teacher teaches virtue, such priorities must be reflected in
the way he assesses students. He may not claim to teach virtue and
then assign one-thousand-word essays wherein students merely recapitulate his lectures.

Boethius offers a common, compelling apologia for his "worldly ambition," which is simply a nice thing to call "fake happiness." He claims
that he engaged in politics "so that virtue should not grow old unpraised," meaning someone must be in charge, and that someone might
as well be a good man. Following Plato, Boethius acknowledges that
good men do not relish the work of governing others, but if good men
do not begrudgingly seek out positions of power, wicked men will rule
the world unchallenged. Given Boethius's anger at having lost all the
material benefits which come from fame, Lady Philosophy is not convinced. Boethius might have begun his career in politics with great zeal
for truth and goodness, but somewhere along the line, he was suckered
into caring more about his reputation and the comforts of his home.

Few students reading *The Consolation* will forthrightly claim they
want fame, renown, and the envy of their peers. On the other hand,

"worldly ambition" needs to be explained to high school students in the most confrontational, vexing manner possible. The student zealous for good grades falls under the umbrella of Lady Philosophy's disdain, for good grades are no more an indication of wisdom than Boethius's condemnation to prison is an indication of his guilt. Good grades lead to scholarships, scholarships lead to more prestigious colleges, prestigious scholarships lead to elite jobs, elite jobs lead to fame, renown, and envy. At no point along the way is a student necessarily virtuous, happy, content, or selfless. Nonetheless, the want of good grades is often defended as a simple matter of prudence, forethought, and responsibility, which is little different than Boethius's defense of his want of power. I have often asked students, "If you found out today that you were never going to pass another examination for the rest of your life—that you would fail every test and quiz you took for the rest of high school, and that you would make it into college on a technicality, and then fail every quiz and test there, as well—how might it come to you as a relief?" I am always astounded to hear students say, "Well, it would mean I wouldn't have to try at school anymore," the assumption being that a failed quiz nullifies the value of an education in virtue. Virtue has no value if it cannot be quantified and entered in a ledger.

Teachers have a hand in fostering these assumptions, though, and so evaluations administered over *The Consolation* need to be carefully constructed to not undercut the thesis of the book. If assessments on *The Consolation* contain multiple choice questions, true and false questions, blanks to be filled in, and rote facts about Boethius's life to be recapitulated, there is little point in reading the book. The final assessment I give on *The Consolation* depends on a later claim of the Lady that the wicked are happier if they are caught and punished than if they get away with their crimes. Every student must write a conversation between himself and Lady Philosophy wherein some sin which the student has lately gotten away with is on the line. The student argues that he is better off not confessing to his parents what he has done, and Lady Philosophy tries to convince him he will be happier coming clean. "You must represent Lady Philosophy's arguments accurately, but tailor them to your particular situation. Put up a zealous fight with her, though. Employ all your powers of reason and rhetoric to get away with your sin. I do not need to know what the sin in question is. You may speak of it vaguely. If you can defeat Lady Philosophy's arguments in favor of confession, fine. That is the end of the matter. You are better off having gotten away with your sin. If you cannot defeat Lady Philosophy's arguments, though, you must confess the sin to your parents. You must show them the dialog you have written and confess the matter to them. Am I asking you to confess your deepest, darkest sin to them? No. But you may not choose some trivial theft committed in the kitchen ten years ago. There should be some sting to it."

The only way for the teacher to prove the merit of such an assignment is to likewise perform it alongside students. Last year, after giving this assignment, I passed out an example of my own.

Having failed to defeat Lady Philosophy's arguments, I informed the secondary administrator at Veritas that I regularly failed to do certain work required of my position as a humanities teacher, but that I had successfully evaded getting caught. If a teacher is in the habit of giving his students assessments which he himself has no interest in completing, he is not truly teaching against "worldly ambition," but asking his students to perform arbitrary work for ephemeral rewards. A good chef is constantly tasting his own cooking. So, too, a good assessment does not merely ensure that the student has been paying attention. Rather, a good assessment offers something of worth to the student in and of itself. God gives us tests not to catch and confirm us in our sin; a test sent from God offers the chance to gain virtue, even if we have not lately been in the habit of seeking virtue. The tests of God can be prepared for, but not crammed for, and neither can the tests of God be cheated on. If the teacher wants to assess students in a manner which does not further worldly ambition, he must strive to test as God tests. Such assessments bridge the classroom with the outside world; such repairs are necessary after the disassociation of school and life which occurs in early adolescence. The high school philosophy teacher is repairing ruins in a way the elementary school teacher is not. Little children love school, and they speak of school naturally and easily, as though school was a thing about the world. When the car windows steam up in November, they recall lessons from science class. Outside the classroom, caterpillars, leaves, sun, moon, stars, water, and dirt confirm lessons and illustrations given by a teacher inside the classroom. The notion that school is about the world, though, dies for a time when a boy or girl passes through puberty, for at such a point (especially for young men) the world becomes about sex, and sex is simply never spoken of in school. Lust becomes the only vice over which a young man truly feels guilt, yet his teachers are typically too cowardly or ashamed to speak of lust in a psychologically realistic manner. While the good teacher claims a good education is about "virtue," the only virtue which a young man thinks truly divine (and worth pursuing) is chastity, for angels alone refrain from constant meditation on women. This might strike some as an odd claim, given that young men often seem desperate to escape chastity, but the shame and confusion suffered over lust is suffered privately, and young men perform elaborate shows for one another to cover over this shame. Once sex becomes the real story of the world (and popular culture is often little more than a priest of Eros), school becomes arbitrary, a series of banal hoops to jump through for the amusement of daft adults who are too dowdy and dull to see the real story. It is the task of the philosophy teacher (the teacher of virtue), however, to recall all the young Nebuchadnezzars from the field of beasts, speak to them with wisdom, charity, and clarity about lust, and to reestablish the classroom as a place where significant, dangerous intellectual labor takes place. To such ends, multiple choice tests will not work.

CHAPTER SIX

On Pleasure

"Of bodily pleasure, I can think of little to say. Its pursuit is full of anxiety and its fulfillment full of remorse. Frequently, like a kind of reward for wickedness, it causes great illness and unbearable pain for those who make it their source of enjoyment. I do not know what happiness lies in its passions, but that the end of pleasure is sorrow is known to everyone who cares to recall his own excesses."
                                        - Lady Philosophy, 3.7 (p. 59)

Nothing in *The Consolation* is more likely to draw charges of Gnosticism than the passages in which the Lady admits she has "little to say" about physical pleasure, specifically the pleasures of sex and food. The Lady never condemns pleasure, but admits forthrightly the matter is of little interest to her, and this distinction is significant, for Lady Philosophy is the creation of a man who is about to die. Boethius's thought on physical pleasure is best understood from this highly particular context. Imagine conducting an interview with St. Polycarp of Smyrna as he was being led in chains to an amphitheater where he would be burned alive. Imagine asking the saint, who was well into his eighties when he was martyred, "What do you think of sexual pleasure?" We would think less of St. Polycarp for wasting his time answering the question than we would if he sighed and brushed the question aside. Or what would we make of the man who received news that a hydrogen bomb would, in a matter of minutes, vaporize his entire city, and responded by running to his refrigerator and eating cold roast beef as quickly as possible? Any sane man would think such a response to imminent death absurd, petty, pathetic, selfish, and such judgments could be made without condemning physical pleasure altogether. The Lady has little interest in mounting an assault on physical pleasure, and neither does she condemn procreation and prosciutto after the fashion of the Gnostics, but she does make a few hasty remarks on pitfalls of seeking pleasure out for its own sake. These comments are germane to the teacher of virtue.

The Lady's dismissal of bestial pleasures recalls Adam's conversations with the archangel Raphael in Milton's *Paradise Lost*. Having looked into the future and seen that man will fall, the Father does not want Adam and Eve trying to excuse their sin later on the grounds they were ill-prepared, uneducated, and unaware of their enemy. The Father sends Raphael to teach the man and woman about the rebellion in heaven, the creation of the universe, and their own personal freedom and power to choose good or evil. Having listened to lengthy discourses from Raphael on history, theology, and philosophy, Adam is only interested in talking of Eve. Little thrills him more than connubial bliss, and he describes for the embarrassed angel his first romp with Eve, how the birds sang and the golden light filtered through the trees. Adam then confesses the wisdom of Eve, his devotion to her, and how nothing makes him happier than taking her to bed. Hearing this, Raphael cautions Adam to not grant greater importance to lesser things. Even animals copulate, the Archangel teaches, but human beings were made greater than animals; the man who exalts sex as his chief delight rejects what is regal and kingly about man in favor of what is common to all beasts.

Similarly, Lady Philosophy is skeptical that any great revelation of God will unfold to the man zealously committed to pleasing his palate or his libido. Americans are uniquely poised (and desperate) to hear this claim, for the quality of American food has risen so dramatically within the last generation, one must wonder how longer such progress is sustainable. One must also wonder what it means. In reading *The Supper of the Lamb*, Robert Farrar Capon's unusual theological cookbook from 1969, one gets a startling picture of the American grocery store from yesteryear. Capon assumes his readers have never seen or tasted fresh ginger, which he suggests most Americans will have to special order, and while Capon is familiar with many exotic and imported varieties of cheese, he laments his readers will only be able to taste foul and funky delights like Taleggio and Époisses on the rarest of occasions, if ever, without travelling to the Continent. Given the manner Capon talks about beer, one can only imagine he has quaffed many Belgian trippels, Belgian wits, much fresh Kölsch from Cologne, and more than a few doppelbocks, eisbocks, and Bavarian weizenbocks in his time, and yet he assumes that the average American finds nothing more than German-American lagers and pilsners on the shelves of his grocery store.

In Richmond, Virginia, where I live, every Tuesday hundreds of people wait for hours in line outside The Veil Brewing Co. to buy four-packs of beer which often cost north of twenty dollars each. Similar scenes may be found outside scores of American breweries every week. Imagine telling a working man in 1994 that, by the time his grandchildren were born, American taste in food and drink would have graduated through successively higher realms of excellence and demand that even the hoi polloi would queue for a whole afternoon just to buy a decent five dollar can of beer. Such changes did not happen overnight, but nearly so. Fifteen years ago, my friends discovered a local wine shop which sold beer from Stone, a rising microbrewery, and one afternoon we all marveled over a five dollar twenty-two-ounce bottle of beer someone splurged on and divvied up six ways. The beer in question was Arrogant Bastard, surely a joke about the ascendance of the American palate. Today, though, I wouldn't deign to spend my daily calories consuming that stuff. Starbucks was thought quite fancy twenty years ago, but is regarded as wholly unremarkable anymore, for better and more costly cups of coffee are easy to come by in any American city. Even middling grocery stores now carry cheeses imported from France, Spain, and Italy, and the cheese selection at the perfectly pedestrian Kroger where I shop regularly features Harbison, a washed-rind cheese made in Vermont which is well over thirty dollars a pound, as well as blue cheese smoked over hazelnuts from the Rogue Creamery in Oregon which sells for forty dollars a pound. The food available to Americans is far more sophisticated and more delicious than it was thirty years ago, and Americans are willing to pay through the nose for it. But arguing that our supermarkets are better is an entirely separate matter from arguing we are ultimately happier because of it.

In the last ten years, I have moved from spending my surplus cash on music to spending it on food and drink. With clarity, I recall attending a potluck at the home of a friend back in 2008, which was just around the time costly cheeses were becoming common in American supermarkets. Someone at the potluck had purchased a large round of Humboldt Fog, Cypress Grove's now ubiquitous soft-ripened goat cheese, and left it on the buffet table. Up until that point in my life, I had never considered cheese. I did not object to cheese and was reasonably fond of it in a hot sandwich, but cheese did not seem a thing worthy of contemplation. After spreading a little Humboldt Fog on a piece of toast, though, and then spreading a little more on another piece of toast, I was sufficiently curious over what exactly I was eating. The Humboldt Fog was not like other cheeses, and seemed worlds apart from the basketball-colored bricks of cheddar sold for pocket change at most grocery stores. Bite by bite, my interest in the party dimmed, and then all others disappeared. There were only two, myself and this peculiar, entrancing being composed of nothing more than milk and time. Over the next hour, I ate the entire twelve ounce round, which was roughly the size and shape of, say, an American Girl doll's birthday cake. Since that day, with every passing year, I have become ever more fond of cheese, ever more willing to spend increasing sums on cheese, and ever more disappointed if I do not have the right cheeses for Pascha, Christmas, Thanksgiving, or Friday.

I have learned a little of God, a little of history, and a little philosophy in my pursuit of the best cheeses, and yet very fine things are capable of creating a kind of mania in their devotees which common things cannot. No man travels to the ends of the earth for mediocre things, or for merely adequate things. Adequate things tend to keep a man's temperament cool, composed, but extreme things call forth extreme responses. To expect a measured response to decadent things is naïve, for I have lavished whole afternoons on driving from grocer to grocer, desperate for some delicacy I have lately read about. While standing in Church, my mind wanders to the guests I will later host, and I muse over the food I am serving and whether it will be good enough, and then I become anxious to leave Church as soon as the service is over so I can attend more grocers and find something truly worthy of the taste I want to be known for. If someday you dine in my home, and if I serve you tuna casserole made from a box, it will mean I have overcome the world.

In no wise should this be taken as a condemnation of pleasant things; however, Lady Philosophy recognizes that once a man seeks satisfaction through physical pleasure, he will both abandon and despise the status quo. He will come to dwell on mundane aspects of life which he formerly let pass by without concern, without care. You are free to go on drinking Folger's Crystals and know no better, or you can risk having a cup of something alarmingly delicious, imported from a tiny farm in Panama, which costs as much per pound as your monthly gas budget. The man who develops fancy taste simply has one more thing to worry about. While I recognize these kinds of claims have an anti-intellectual air, I mean merely to say that pleasure is no way of gaining an advantage over the world. The man who thinks little of his coffee, pays little for his coffee, and drinks his coffee with simplicity of heart is not worse off than the man who thinks much of his coffee, sacrifices much for his coffee, and whose every mug is attended by a great fuss over nuance and perfection of form. Both the gourmand and the simpleton take part in separate economies of time, pleasure, and care, neither of which is ultimately better than the other.

A man cannot satisfy his desire for fine things without simultaneously expanding that desire, and with the expansion of any want comes with deeper suffering. Want is unpleasant. What is true of fine things is also true of art which appeals to the senses but not the soul. Fine things are only safe in the company of others, for company makes luxury allowable, but there is something hopelessly vulgar about drinking a fine bottle of wine all by yourself. Nothing degrades physical pleasure quite like the lonely pursuit of it. Consider, for a moment, two young men talking about the latest summer blockbuster, some run-of-the-mill billion dollar special effects affair with alluring costumes, monsters, spaceships, and the destruction of New York City. In conversation, fans of the film are often given to saying, "The part where such-and-such takes place is amazing," or, "The scene where so-and-so kills such-a-one is fantastic." When these exchanges take place, neither speaker is representing his thoughts on the film. Rather, each speaker is trying to present the film once again. But there is really nothing to say about the film, so they are simply trying (and failing) to watch the film again in words. The conversation is a little vexing, though, because they are not having a good time discussing the film, but remembering what a good time they had watching the film. What they are doing is not terribly different than popping in a DVD of the film and seeing it a second time. To present the film again with mere words is unsatisfying, though, because no amount of pure discussion can match the sensual experience of seeing the film, and so such conversations often conclude with resolutions to see the film again soon. For this reason, a big deal is made of the release of blockbusters, and some stores stay open until midnight on the release date so the film can be seen again as quickly as possible. Seeing the film again quickly is the best way to fill the awkward intellectual silence which the film creates. On the other hand, two people talking about intellectually satisfying films like *Paths of Glory* or *Magnolia* are generally not saying, "The part where… was awesome," and not because they believe the film is without awesome moments, but because their conversation aims not to present the film again, but to represent the film, recreate the film, resurrect the film as a more perfect and glorious story. A conversation about *Magnolia* is also far more likely to be filled with questions like "Did you notice…?" or "What did so-and-so mean when he said…?"

Sensual art prompts few questions. On the other hand, I have been speaking with friends about *Magnolia* off and on ever since I saw the film in 1999, and I've probably had more conversations about the film in the last five years than in the ten which followed my first viewing, though I haven't seen Magnolia since I married (and gave one of my daughters Magnolia as a middle name) and I don't have plans to see it again anytime soon. Thinking about the film does not inspire within me a desire to see it, but rather to talk about it more and hear others talk about it. *Magnolia* is around three hours long, and I would much rather talk with my friends about the film for three hours than watch it again. Imagine two people trying to sustain a conversation about the third Transformers movie, *Dark of the Moon*, for 157 minutes, the total running time of the film.

There may not seem like much of a connection between banal amusements like Transformers movies and the pleasures of fine wine, yet fine wine is reduced to brute, sensual gratification if it is sought for its own sake. When fine things are produced to contribute gravity, solemnity, and dignity to a feast or holy day, the real pleasure of those fine things is enjoyed in the qualities of personhood which they draw out of the human beings who eat and drink them. The memory of excellent things is actually the recollection of the honored Other. When pleasurable things are enjoyed for their own sake, the memory of those things quickly comes to taunt us and will go on taunting us until we seize them again.

Boethius was a husband and a father, but when the Lady hastily comments on the beguiling pleasures of sex, she does not assume unchastity or infidelity. When Christians discuss the dangers and enticements of sexual pleasure they are typically minded to caution one another about adultery, lust, and fornication, though Lady Philosophy does not name these as entrapments of sexual pleasure. Even the married man can enslave his soul to the sexual pleasures offered by his wife; the fact that neither sex nor fine foods are wrong in and of themselves hardly means they may be enjoyed casually, wantonly, or indiscriminately. The loftier the pleasure, the more needful it is that pleasure submit to some higher spiritual rite. In his biography of St. Francis, Chesterton writes:

> ...*sex cannot be admitted to a mere equality among elementary emotions or experiences like eating and sleeping. The moment sex ceases to be a servant it becomes a tyrant. There is something dangerous and disproportionate in its place in human nature, for whatever reason; and it does really need a special purification and dedication.*

The "disproportionate" power sex holds over the human imagination means we may liken sexual desire to a gale force wind which might swiftly deliver a little boat home, but if the rudder of that boat is ever-so-slightly directed off course, the sailor will lose his way quickly, not gradually. St. Paul's declaration that "it is better to marry than to burn with lust" (1 Cor. 7:9) by no means vindicates every sexual proclivity of a husband merely because he directs his lust toward his wife. Like every other desire, sexual desire must be tamed, and resisting temptations to fornication and adultery are hardly the full extent of this taming. If sex comes to rule the imagination of a man, he should expect old age to be an overwhelming vexation, for the soul is fully capable of longing for things which the body is no longer capable of giving to it.

During those rare passages of my life wherein I draw near to God, resist temptation with ease, and say my prayers with sincerity and simplicity of heart, my piety is principally staked in an ongoing conversation with God which occurs just below a conscious level. Even while I am teaching, reading, watching a film, cooking, or conversing, my mind and heart flicker with words, thoughts, hopes, and fears that are offered up to God, and God answers merely by receiving them. The place in my heart from whence arise these prayers is always active, but rarely committed to holy things.

Often, I give my students their exams weeks before they are due. I tell them, "You may not be actively working on this exam for a week, but I want the essay questions from the exam hanging around in the back of your head." Issues of profound importance descend beneath our conscious thought life, and our souls go to work on them, hammering them out, turning them over, testing them, meditating on them. In the authoring of this book, I often revisited a chapter from *The Consolation* in the morning, even if I was not planning on writing about the passage until the evening. Over the course of the day, my thoughts would often return to the passage a thousand times, even if only for a fraction of a second. By the evening, I found the text had arrived at fresh clarity in my absence from it. Of course, it is a rare passage in my life wherein I am capable of devoting this obscure, yet productive aspect of my soul to God, for this aspect of my soul is typically preoccupied with issues of physical pleasure. I do not mean that my mind is preoccupied with the friendships which arise over sharing fine food, and I do not mean my mind is preoccupied with the bond of marriage, or the new life which emerges from sexual union. I mean that place just below conscious thought is usually slaving away at plans to please "that most worthless and brittle master, the human body" (p. 60).

"The pleasures derived from a wife and children are indeed most honest; but there is a story all too natural that a certain man found his children tormentors. How painful the condition of every such man is, there is no need to remind you, since you have experienced such conditions yourself, and are still not free from anxiety. So I agree with my Euripides when he said that the childless man was fortunate in his misfortune."
- Lady Philosophy, 3.7 (p. 60)

Upon reading such words, we must keep in mind that Lady Philosophy is not teaching that "It is good for a man not to have sexual relations with a woman" (1 Cor. 7:1), as St. Paul does, but that neither marriage nor children should be sought for the pleasure they offer, even while the pleasures derived from family life are "most honest." Christians are still quite embarrassed to talk about sex, and a great many young men go the altar without receiving much advice from older men on the subject. The need for chastity before marriage is a common topic, however, so far as the need for prudence and moderation after marriage, we are silent. I have even heard older Christians tell young men, "When you are married, you may have as much sex as you like. Until then, you must wait," which more or less makes chastity a kind of trial which must be endured for the sake of sexual pleasure. While there is nothing wrong with admitting that chastity is unpleasant, and that certain pleasures of marriage are a reward for patience, sex must be the means to something greater or else sexual appetite will become a tyrant. We would never tell a young man, "When you are twenty-one, you may have as much gin as you like. Until then, you must wait."

A dignified, humane approach to pleasure is not possible without first articulating a proper relationship between the body and the soul. In response to the moral relativism which was common to the 1970s and 1980s, many American Christians adopted the stance that every free act of a man was either sinful or not-sinful. For nearly two generations now, we have refused to delineate between an act which is allowable and an act which is commendable. Accordingly, we believe there is no difference between paying ten dollars to see a movie and giving ten dollars to a homeless man outside the theater. These are morally equivalent actions, so far as we are concerned. Moviegoing is not-sinful, charity is not-sinful, and there is no way of distinguishing between the two. In claiming this, modern Christians are able to avoid one of their least favorite subjects, shallowness, for the refusal by Christians to believe certain acts are morally neutral is largely responsible for the vacuous, vapid, ephemeral quality of Christian culture today.

In 1 Corinthians 6:12, St. Paul acknowledges that some things might be "lawful," but not "helpful," although Christians are likewise terrified that certain deeds are spiritually "helpful," because it means we might *have* to do them. The idea that giving to the poor is spiritually helpful is quite anxiety-inducing for people who retreat to the mantra of "saved by faith, not works" any time a sermon begins to smart a little. Seeing the third Transformers movie might be lawful, but it will not help your soul. Praying, fasting, and giving alms will do you good, though: spiritual good, which is precisely why we do not like to do them. Spiritual goods do not please the body, that brittle master, and when the body is not getting its due, it complains against the spirit.

Our confusion over pleasure is also derived from confusion about the Incarnation. As the Western world inclines towards Etsy, organic food, gardening, craft beer, homemade bread, and speaks evermore dismissively of mass-produced goods, there comes a temptation to make the Incarnation nothing more than a theological proof for the zeitgeist—as though the Son being born of a virgin is "earthy," and so we ought to buy local. There is a certain kind of Christian so desperate to prove he is not gnostic that he lacks the common sense to admit that, even while the internet carries Pastor Steve's sermons to the people of Uganda, the internet has simply not proven to be worth the headache, temptation, and corruption which it has also brought. The Incarnation vindicates the goodness of material things, but the Incarnation is not proof that all men are free to manipulate nature however they choose. The Incarnation teaches us that rocks, rivers, rabbits, mountains, and trees are good, but the Incarnation does not prove the goodness of iPhones or Facebook anymore than it proves the goodness of crystal meth, the morning after pill, or a stack of dirty magazines. While Christians are quick to claim that no tool can be evil in and of itself, the new converts to Christianity described in Acts 19 burned all their books of magic. They did not try to reinterpret principles of sorcery in light of the Resurrection, and they did not look for Gospel themes in theories of alchemy. They did not try to reclaim and redeem witchcraft, neither did they find some new and more appropriate purpose for the books, like using them for doorstops, or writing on the backs of the pages. While it is not illogical to imagine a book being used as a mere physical object, it was nonetheless untenable for new converts to keep their books of magic close at hand for allegedly noble or neutral uses.

The Lady's dismissal of pleasure is likely to earn sighs from readers who have read Robert Farrar Capon's *The Supper of the Lamb* or seen the film *Babette's Feast*, touch points in recent Christian conversations about God, pleasure, and asceticism. Both Capon and Babette are concerned with fine things, the goodness of the world, and what God wants to teach us about Himself in the delights offered by nature. While both view a sensuous meal as a "love feast," Capon and Babette also have far more to say about renunciation than the average American is comfortable with.

> *As long as the passion goes on, we are called to share it as we can—especially if, by the mere luck of the draw, we have escaped the worst pains of it. Do all you can to help, of course; but don't, for all that, forget that you are also called simply to bear. In the end, the agony lies too deep for any cure except the cross. Fast, therefore, until His*

Passion brings the world home free. He works through any crosses He can find. In a time of affluence, fasting may well be the simplest one of all. (Capon, p. 146)

The poor man may envy the rich their houses, their lands, and their cars; but given a good wife, he rarely envies them their table. The rich man dines festally, but unless he is an exceptional lover of being—unless he has the soul of a poet and a saint—his feasts are too often only single: They delight the palate, but not the intellect. They are greeted with a deluxe but mindless attention: "What was it, dear, sirloin or porterhouse?" (Capon, p. 25)

Capon's reference to a banal inability to distinguish which fine thing has just been enjoyed, or rather the boredom and sad inattentiveness ultimately engendered in the man wholly accustomed to only the best and highest pleasures, is simply that "end of pleasure" which is "sorrow" (p. 59). Great physical pleasures cannot be enjoyed without some cost, and thus pleasure is always purchased at the expense of some new anxiety, dependency, or frustration. Most men who have ever sincerely declared a love of whiskey have also, at another time, doubly sworn hatred of the stuff.

Unlike Gnostics, Christians affirm the goodness of both body and soul. Gnostics only affirm the goodness of the soul. However, in affirming that both body and soul are good, Christians by no means set body and soul on equal footing. The body is good, but the soul is more important. In St. Matthew's Gospel (16:25), Christ teaches that, "Whoever would save his life will lose it, but whoever loses his life for my sake will find it." The life which a man loses for Christ is simply the life which Christ loses for us, His physical life. The life found in Christ is the life of the soul. He who lives by the sword of the flesh will die by the sword of the Spirit, but he who lives by the sword of the Spirit will die by the sword of the flesh. In Book XIV of the *City of God*, St. Augustine distinguishes between "the carnal man" and "the spiritual man":

> *When, therefore, man lives according to man, not according to God,*
> *he is like the Devil. Because not even an angel might live according*
> *to an angel, but only according to God, if he was to abide in the truth,*
> *and speak God's truth and not his own lie . . . When, then, a man*
> *lives according to the truth, he lives not according to himself, but ac-*
> *cording to God... When, therefore, man lives according to himself—*
> *that is, according to man, not according to God—assuredly he lives*
> *according to a lie; not that man himself is a lie, for God is his author*
> *and creator, who is certainly not the author and creator of a lie, but*
> *because man was made upright, that he might not live according to*
> *himself, but according to Him that made him... the source of man's*
> *happiness lies only in God, whom he abandons when he sins, and not*
> *in himself...*

Augustine explains that the carnal man has a spirit, but his spirit serves the body. A man whose natures are properly ordered will subject his body to the rule of the spirit, and so the body serves the interests of the spirit; when a spiritual man is given the choice of blaspheming Christ or living a day longer, the body humbly dies for the sake of the spirit.

The greater importance of the soul means that man should not attempt to ornament himself with physical beauty, but spiritual. "Fortune can never make yours what Nature has made alien to you" (p. 49) teaches the Lady, which means a man can bring the beauty of Nature near Himself, but never incorporate the beauty of nature into his own being. The Lady claims that "if clothing catches my eye, my admiration will be directed at either the quality of the material or the skill of the tailor." The man who embraces this idea would, upon seeing a woman who had spent hours getting ready for a dinner date, not say, "You look beautiful," but rather, "Your dress and your blush and your necklace are beautiful."

If his wife dabbed Chanel on her neck, he would not say, "You smell ravishing," but, "Your perfume smells ravishing." The soul transcends the body, and thus it is vain to "decorate" the soul with material baubles. An ornament is something which is more beautiful than the thing it ornaments; we bedeck Christmas trees with lights and colors, not with lumps of coal, for lumps of coal are less luminous and dazzling than a naked pine. If a lump of coal was to prove a genuine ornament of another thing, that thing would have to be less glorious than coal. In like manner, golden earrings are not as glorious as a woman and so they cannot prove a genuine ornament. Neither is physical beauty more glorious than spiritual beauty, and so the virtuous woman who pours herself into a slinky dress for a cocktail party, the Lady insinuates, loses her beauty, for those who see her are drawn to what is lesser.

> **"Fortune can never make yours what Nature has made alien to you... From all this it is obvious that not one of those things which you count among your blessings is in fact any blessing of your own at all. And if, then, they contain a spark of beauty worth seeking, why weep over their loss or rejoice at their preservation? If Nature gives them their beauty, how does it involve you?"**
> **- Lady Philosophy, 2.5 (p. 34-35)**

While Lady Philosophy dismisses the idea that physical beauty or wealth can change the being of the person who possess them, men try to incorporate a diverse range of Fortune's benefits into their nature. Consider two young Star Wars fans trying to one-up the other so far as love of the Force is concerned:

Tom: I've seen every Star Wars movie ten times.
Dick: I've seen every Star Wars movie ten times and I own all of them on DVD.
Tom: I own all of them on DVD and I have the Millenium Falcon

Lego set.

Dick: I own copies of the Return of the Jedi *script.*

Tom: My copy of that script is autographed by George Lucas.

Dick: Well, I wrote the script. It's actually a documentary about my life.

Every December I ask students to make Christmas wish lists, which I hang around the classroom for a few weeks. Most students write down a few things they actually want, then devolve into farfetched desires for Italian sports cars and fancy girlfriends. One year, a student turned in a list which sounded something like this:

1. *Lebron James rookie card.*
2. *Playstation 3*
3. *Lebron James replica jersey.*
4. *Lebron James autograph.*
5. *iTunes gift card.*
6. *Lebron James as my personal bodyguard.*
7. *A door that leads into the brain of Lebron James which I can freely enter and exit at will.*
8. *The power to destroy Lebron James' body and soul in Hell.*
9. *More iTunes gift cards (may or may not give them to Lebron James)*

Freud would have had a heyday with such a document. As a philosophy teacher, I nearly did, as well. I was struck by the ever-mounting intensity of the boy's desired proximity with the object of his affection, and the humorous despair in the eighth item, in which the horrific vanity of the want to possess a thing is revealed. The boy went from a position of adoration, seeking first the icon of his beloved, then wanting the jersey, which could make him look like his beloved, and then the autograph of the beloved, a relic of the saint which could be venerated.

The great turn in the list takes place between the fourth item and the sixth, wherein Lebron James goes from being an idol to a slave. The enslavement of the beloved takes on divine qualities in the seventh and eighth items, wherein the boy longs for a godlike power which can be used to know the beloved from within, to move passed the gates of Lebron James' metaphysical autonomy into the realm of his person. Every desire is the desire to become. For this reason, all earthly desires are tinged with tragedy, for there are only two things a man can ultimately become: god and nothing.

The only earthly relationship which approximates our relationship with God is marriage, wherein a man and woman become one another in their children. The husband yields his person that his wife might possess it, the wife yields her person that the husband might possess it, and the child born of such mutual yielding is the indivisible icon of two persons. Still, even marriage is fraught with the perils which attend a failure to truly possess and yield to anything less than God, for even if husband and wife become "one flesh" when making love, they nonetheless part when they are finished and return to their separate realms of being. While it is crass to think of husband and wife "owning" one another, the vexing ultimate inability of husband and wife to possess the other (in body or soul) points us beyond earthly relationships to the only Other which we can ever become, or ever finally surrender to.

All being drafts on the being of God, and no being is underived but the being of God. If every desire is the desire to become, only God can finally satisfy. Having seen the film and read the book, little boys pretend to be Robin Hood, and little girls pretend to be Maid Marian, but the Divine alone allows all those who truly love Him to become one with Him. The man who reads the Gospel and lives like Christ is not so different from the eighth-grade ballplayer who says, "I'm Kobe," or the little Star Wars fan who says, "I'm Luke." But the Divine shares His divinity, His nature, in a way nothing else can. "I have been crucified with Christ. It is no longer I who live, but Christ who lives in me," writes St.

Paul to the Galatians (2:20), and when St. John the Baptist sees Christ, he declares, "He must increase, but I must decrease" (John 3:30).

Personhood is one of God's greatest gifts to man, for personhood is that which God allows us to return to Himself in exchange for salvation.

> **"Fame, in fact, is a shameful thing,**
> **and so often deceptive."**
> **- Lady Philosophy, 3.6 (p. 58)**

In the era of social media, fame has become nearly as common and omnipresent a pleasure as sex and food. Given what care we invest not only in food, but in photographing and presenting our food, Americans might just derive more pleasure for being famous for eating good food than from the taste of the food itself. Perhaps a restaurant will someday open wherein people pay to have their photo taken next to opulent plates of sushi or sublimely cosmetic crown lamb roasts, even while they are not allowed to eat from them.

Lady Philosophy speaks of fame several times. In Book 2, she merely remarks fame is relative, that no one is quite so famous as they think, and that the same things which make a man famous in his own country make him despised in another country. The inverse is also true, for Christ teaches that "a prophet is not without honor except in his hometown and among his relatives and in his own household" (Mark 6:4). The Lord is here at his most Solomonic, for He sounds weary, bemused, and annoyed that so many people who know Him best revere Him least. When the prophet arrives in a foreign city where he is unknown and speaks on behalf of God, the people will listen, for the prophet sprung fully formed from the forehead of Zeus, for all they know. Back home, however, the prophet's grade school teachers find it hard to accept him as the mouthpiece of the Almighty, for they recall how he flunked fourth grade, how his voice cracked in middle school, and how he wept like a baby when Brooke Hawkins turned him down for prom. As *The Consolation* progresses, though, the Lady moves from claiming Fortune will not help a man to claiming fame will do him real harm. "Many, indeed, are the men who have wrongly acquired fame through the false opinions of the people…" says the Lady, "And even if the praise is deserved, it cannot add anything to the philosopher's feeling: He measures happiness not by popularity, but by the true voice of his own conscience" (p. 58). As a pathetic, fame-seeking pseudo-intellectual and sophist, these cautions ring true.

Lest I get ahead of myself, I should readily own up to the fact that I am not a famous person. Nonetheless, social media has rendered fame cheap, democratic, and some of the articles and essays I have written for the CiRCE Institute (where I began writing in 2013) have been well received and enjoyed wider circulation. This moderate success comes at the end of a decade-long search for an audience. Fourteen years ago, I began a blog wherein I collected my thoughts on theology and popular culture for a small group of friends. A few strangers and acquaintances occasionally populated the comments section. I rarely received more than fifty hits a day, though I checked often, those fifty hits were precious to me, and I thrilled when something I wrote was linked or referenced by a more well-known blogger and I picked up a hundred hits.

As an aside, I should remark that I accidentally deleted the entire blog one day by accident, and thousands of articles and odd thoughts which had slowly and patiently accumulated over the years were suddenly lost. At the time this happened, I was panicked, angry, and cursing my luck and stupidity. However, had I not accidentally deleted the blog, I would have gone back and intentionally done so years later after I began writing for CiRCE, because the blog was theological juvenilia, philosophic doggerel, a sequence of banal and speciously thoughtful reflections on the world. Thank God I never became well known for anything I wrote on those early blogs. Back in the day, I would have given great sums for my work to obtain a large audience, and today I would give a great sum for those articles to fall down an endless black hole. The things we want to be known for in our twenties are the things we are ashamed of in our thirties.

After I met Andrew Kern in late 2013, I submitted an article on classical education to the CiRCE blog and, lo and behold, a day after it was published, eighteen people had clicked "like" at the bottom. At the time, this seemed an outrageous success. A crown of laurels would not be too gaudy a decoration to adorn the brow of the man who opened his thoughts up to seven billion potential readers and enjoyed the moderate praise of .000000000257 of that audience.

Over the next year, I wrote fifty more articles. With each, I assiduously and hourly checked the response. Eventually, I wrote something which collected fifty likes, a hundred likes, two hundred, five hundred. By the time I was writing articles which might receive five hundred likes, I was aware that certain subjects were bound for wider readership. A long, dense essay explaining Remi Brague's anthropological cosmology might take hours to write, but few people would read it. Never mind that it would be personally beneficial for me to explain myself carefully and patiently, and never mind that such an article might be a great help for someone researching Ptolemy. Within a year of having my first essay published on the CiRCE blog, the idea of writing something that only eighteen people would like seemed a complete waste of time.

However, the absurdity of such dependence on human praise is regularly confirmed to me. Readers regularly like and share articles wherein I argue one thing, and then they share and praise articles arguing the opposite of what I have claimed. Were I a real philosopher (or a good person), I would not care one way or the other, for the Lady claims that "even when fame is deserved, it cannot add anything to the philosopher's feelings" (p. 58).

While some excitement attends the publication of a well-received essay, wider readership opens the author up to praise and censure alike. I have been lauded by strangers on the internet, and I have been condemned by them; censure always hurts more than praise feels good. The conquering hero who addresses himself to a thousand hands raised in adoration, yet spies one lone middle finger raised aloft at the back of the crowd, will depart the stage confused and angry. Simian mockery and apt, withering critiques alike have tempted me on many occasions to quit writing altogether. Having blogged for years and spoken at numerous classical education conferences, the authoring of a book was the next natural step in my career. This book will, perhaps, enjoy more committed, interested readers than anything I have written before, although this also means my ideas will be held up to greater scrutiny. Should anyone deign to review this book, and should I read a review which is anything less than unctuous veneration, I will likely come away from the whole project possessed of a pathetic spirit of self-defense. Earlier, Lady Philosophy claims that, "No man is so completely happy that something somewhere does not clash with his condition" (p. 30). If fame enlarges a man's happiness, fame also enlarges that "something, somewhere" which clashes with his condition. As Solomon notes in Ecclesiastes, no man can ever gain an advantage over the world, and neither can anyone gain an advantage over Fortune. "A generation goes, and a generation comes, but the earth remains forever" (Ecc. 1:4). Life itself cannot be strong-armed, and neither can life be gamed forever. Rather, Lady Fortune is always recalibrating the economy of pleasure and pain by which a man negotiates his soul against his station in the world. The more she gives, the more she demands.

"No man is so completely happy that something somewhere does not clash with his condition."
- Lady Philosophy, 2.4 (p. 30)

"C ount your blessings," teaches Lady Philosophy. Fortune has turned on Boethius, though not completely, and he still enjoys many blessings which other men would die for. Even in prison, Fortune offers him a few pleasures. Boethius still has the memory of his past glory to console him in his present suffering, and if Boethius "reckons up the score" of his luck, he has come out on top. Even on death row, the Lady suggests, his noble father-in-law is still alive and his wife has not abandoned him for another man. His sons are yet virtuous. There are plenty of men who would rather die than see their wives prove unfaithful; the cuckolded man would gladly trade places with Boethius.

Do these claims help? A little, although Boethius tells the Lady that some of her words are sweet, but that "as soon as your words stop sounding in [my] ears, the mind is weighed down again." When a man is sick at heart, he is free to count his blessings, but the counting of blessings is not a sustainable solution to human misery. If a man is grieved and wants the aid of God, the last thing he should do is count his blessings, lest he become distracted from his suffering and forget to lift his needs up to God. We tell those who are melancholic or depressed to count their blessings because we do not want to suffer with them, or because their suffering is inappropriate to the occasion. If a man is in a good humor and looking to drink wine, listen to Django Reinhardt, and relax after a hard week at work, the last thing he wants is his sad friend ruining a light, leisurely mood. The sad man is a nuisance to the man in a jovial mood, but if the jovial man can get the sad man to forget his trouble for a moment, the jovial man may go back to having a good time without feeling guilty. "Count your blessings" often carries a subtle accusation of ingratitude, as well. When the happy man tells the sad man to count his blessings, he implies that Christians are bound by laws of piety to smile, and that anything less than delight with the world makes a man a grumbler and a complainer. There is a certain kind of Christian so uncomfortable with spiritual anguish, it is not hard to imagine him chastising Christ on the Cross for uttering the cry of dereliction. Come on! Buck up! You've still got your mother here with you. And your friend John. It's not all bad. Count your blessings.

"Count your blessings" is sometimes treated as a loose interpretation of St. Paul's teaching to "rejoice in the Lord always," but the two sayings have little in common. The "blessings" referred to in "Count your blessings" are usually the blessings of Fortune. When a man loses his house, his friends tell him, "You still have your car." When that man loses his car, his friends say, "You still have your wife." When his wife abandons him, his friends say, "You still have your health." These are not blessings exclusive to the righteous, for even a wicked man may console himself in such a manner. In Acts 5, the apostles were scourged by the Sanhedrin and "left the council, rejoicing that they were counted worthy to suffer dishonor for the name." This is rejoicing in the Lord, not in the comforts of luck. The apostles were happy they had suffered for God, not happy in spite of their suffering. When Christ is crucified, He refuses myrrh, a drug that would alleviate His pain, because He did not want to escape His pain, but to enter as deeply as possible into it.

Granted, what I offer here on the subject of counting your blessings has, at first blush, nothing to do with what the Lady offers Boethius. However, what I find most helpful about these passages on the numbering of blessings is how early in the book they come. Ours is a generation chiefly minded to make Christianity a "positive, encouraging" religion wherein even the somber dignity of the funeral has been replaced with a festive, celebratory event characterized by nostalgic stories, laughter, and a fondly shed tear. The funeral has largely been scrapped, and memorial services are little different than rehearsal dinners.

In fact, the Lady's claim that Boethius still has a little good luck might not be entirely genuine, and she may be testing him with the claim to see if he is shallow enough to take comfort in it. Whether the Lady hopes Boethius buys her point or not, she nonetheless hits an impasse and turns to the subject of other people's misfortune, and here she begins to unveil some of her most Solomonic proverbs.

"No man is so completely happy that something somewhere does not clash with his condition," claims Philosophy (p. 30). Rich men wish they were beautiful. Beautiful men wish they were rich. Famous men want to be left alone, lonely men want companionship. "There is something in the case of each of us that escapes the notice of the man who has not experienced it, but causes horror to the man who has", says the Lady, subtly implying envy is always a failure of imagination (p. 31). We envy men who have the things we want, but we do not often see the suffering, anxiety, and temptation which comes with possessing those things. The rich worry their friends are false. God does not give with both hands, as the saying goes, and so neither the tears nor the opinions of the beautiful are taken seriously, and powerful men live in fear of being attacked. These observations are pedestrian enough, though hard to remember in the moment of temptation. What is more, the rise of social media has seen Americans ever more incredulous that successful people have genuine problems. Within the last decade, "first world problems" has become a proverb spoken caustically to anyone who complains about the occasional mild discomforts of living in a wealthy capitalist society. Long line at the bank? First world problems. No vegan options on the buffet? First world problems. Dumped via text? First world problems. Upon first glance, the woman whining on Facebook that there are no coconut oil potato chips at Whole Foods might seem worthy of nothing more than a slap in the face from Lady Philosophy. But the Lady would not acknowledge the existence of "first world problems," only problems.

This might seem antithetical to the teaching that "He who hath much, wants much," for the poor children in Africa have little, want little, and is not want the source of all human suffering? However, the

Lady claims there is not a man alive who "finds it easy to accept the lot Fortune has sent him" (p. 31). The real problem with a long line at the bank has nothing to do with time, but temptation, for impatience is a sin and the fruit of sin is death. A man might go to Hell for failing to properly address his first world problems, and thus the "first-worldness" of his problems is passing, but the "problems" aspect is eternal. When wealth is absent from a ghetto, jealousy is not, for Fortune gives one poor man a wife, but no wife to another. Fortune gives beauty to one poor woman, but not another. Fortune gives a healthy child to one poor family, but not to another. The Devil is an equal opportunity employer, and does not discriminate based on social standing, and scores of men who live enviable lives nonetheless end their own lives.

Had Boethius lived in our day, he would have spent the first for-ty-four years of his life knowing only first world problems, but as his life closes, he finds death, longing, and evil are universal problems. The original human problem might be seen as a first world problem, then, for the Devil incited a King and Queen who lived in a terrestrial par-adise to do nothing more than nibble a forbidden snack. Hiroshima, Auschwitz, and the Cambodian Killing Fields came from such humble origins. "First world problems" indeed. Lady Philosophy suggests the ambient nature of temptation when she says that "nothing is miserable except when you think it so," for every kind of evil and suffering is en-compassed in this nothing. Christ Himself was similarly universal when He taught "Sufficient for the day is its own trouble" (Matt. 6:34), for He directed this claim to one particular, and thus addressed both rich and poor alike, beautiful and ugly alike. While the poor man may have more trouble than the rich, the rich man has "sufficient" trouble merely because he is human.

In the early chapters of *The Consolation*, Boethius hears a host of the maxims and proverbs which all Westerners are generally aware of to this day. Lady Philosophy works many variations on "Count your blessings" and "Things could always be worse," which are both true, but ultimately ineffectual in satisfying Boethius's complaint against his own bad luck. Many of the consolations the Lady offers Boethius are not explicitly Christian or even theistic, but merely rational. The rational consolations will take an immediate effect on Boethius and quell his anger, but not put his concerns about evil to rest. Strangely enough, these same ineffectual consolations are common to Christians of our day when speaking with suffering friends. "There are plenty of fish in the sea," a Christian mother tells her heartbroken son, though an atheist mother could say the same thing. We often treat rational, natural consolations as the final word on the matter. Or else we say, "You were not selected valedictorian, but you are still graduating with high honors, are you not? You are attending the college you wanted, right?" When such advice is reduced to its philosophical essence, it little more than "Count your blessings when you are sad. You'll feel better." Isn't that what you want? But if it is not best for the body to always be pleased, then neither is it best for the soul to always be pleased.

Given that the Lady believes Boethius's soul will survive his death, when he dies is not actually of much concern to her. Rational and natural consolations only make sense when death is not in the immediate future, for rational consolations direct our attention from what is unpleasant to what is pleasant, and the looming immanence of death tends to make pleasant things seem trite. In America, our consolation in times of material loss is typically hope for greater material gain, and so when a man loses his job, his friends are apt to tell him, "I am sure God has something even better in store for you." Or when a young woman's fiancé unexpectedly calls things off, her friends say, "God has someone even better for you out there." However, were Lady Philosophy to tell Boethius that God has something in store for him which is better than his life back in Rome, it would ring false. The young woman suddenly unengaged has a reasonable expectation of long life ahead, and the same is true for a man in his forties who must seek out a new career, but Boethius is slated to die soon. The blank slate of the future has become small enough that very little may be written on it. Is it possible he will get a reprieve from his sentence at the last second? Of course. And it is possible the young woman will find a better man, as well, and that the unemployed man will find a better job. But it is also possible that none of these things will happen, and everyone knows this. We have all heard tragic stories of suffering wherein a man's material prosperity dried up suddenly and completely while he was yet young, and a family of four went from the penthouse of middle class all the way down to the basement. The "better things" God had in store for such people were not material goods, but spiritual.

As a shallow person, I am often terrified that God has genuinely better things in store for me, for I know that genuinely better things typically come at the expense of pleasurable things. Treasure in heaven comes at the price of treasure on earth, and I love the pleasant things of earth so much, I have little to look forward to when I die. Earthly pleasure can lead to sanctification and epiphany, and we should "taste and see the Lord is good" (Psa. 34:8), as the Psalmist says; however, seeing "the Lord is good" is not the result of every taste, and an over-abundance of tasting distracts from our ability to see the Lord is good. All tasting must be done in such a way that we see the goodness of the Lord, not merely the goodness of his gifts. Obsession with the gift is contempt for the gift-giver.

CHAPTER SEVEN

On Metaphysics and Freedom

"If you try to hoard money, you will have to take it by force. If you want to be resplendent in the dignities of high office, you will have to grovel before the man who bestows it . . . The sleek looks of beauty are fleeting and transitory, more ephemeral than the blossom in spring."
-Lady Philosophy, 3.8 (p. 60-61)

"I do indeed see that sufficiency has nothing to do with riches, or power with kingship, respect with honours, glory with fame, or happiness with pleasures... The reason is very clear. That which is one and undivided is mistakenly subdivided and removed by men from the state of truth and perfection to a state of falseness and imperfection."
-Lady Philosophy, 3.9 (p .63)

The Lady and Boethius agree that "wealth, position, power, fame" and "pleasure" (p. 49) make for happiness, but after examining each, they find that pursuing just one aspect of happiness cuts a man off from the other aspects of happiness. The Lady has not shown that pleasure is bad, but that the man who uses pleasure to reach happiness will find himself divided. The obese man seeks happiness through eating, but eating confirms his obesity and so the pleasure of food is tinged with regret. The man who seeks happiness through having children finds such happiness purchased with fear for their safety. While pleasure is good, pleasure is also a slippery, unsustainable reason for doing anything. Earthly things are ephemeral, fading, finite, and every material road to happiness invariably doubles back on itself. Retaining a horde of money requires brute force to secure it, and thus cash cannot make a man self-sufficient.

Securing a high office means groveling. The more powerful the man, paradoxically, the more necessary it is for him to have a security detail. A man or woman might marry a stunningly beautiful or handsome spouse, and yet beauty is also a liability. While having a lot of money empowers a man to purchase pleasant things, cash proves insufficient company in enjoying them. Despite his great wealth and power, Solomon laments the lack of a single honest woman with whom he can share his kingdom (Ecc. 7:28). The pleasure of achieving good grades leads to the fear of losing them. The pleasures of an affair lead to anxiety of getting caught. "Give strong drink to the one who is perishing, and wine to those in bitter distress; let them drink and forget their poverty and remember their misery no more," (Prov. 31) writes Solomon, although the man who drinks enough to forget his problems will doubtless remember his worries in sickness the morning after. Unless a man figures out how to simultaneously pursue all five paths to happiness at the same time, he will never achieve any real happiness.

"Sufficiency, power, glory, reverence, and happiness" (p. 64) are not separate things, teaches Lady Philosophy, but the same thing considered from five different perspectives. God alone possesses every characteristic of happiness which men long for, though, "Human perversity... makes divisions of that which by nature is one and simple, and in attempting to obtain part of something which has no parts, succeeds in getting neither the part—which is nothing—nor the whole, which they are not interested in" (p. 64). Seeking reverence apart from happiness, or seeking sufficiency but not glory, is no less absurd than the man who is infatuated with his wife's eyes and accordingly plucks them out and takes them on a business trip because he cannot bear to be without them. Some things cannot be edited without being destroyed. While sufficiency, power, glory, reverence, and happiness are all characteristics of perfect human satisfaction, a man must have all of them or none. He may not choose them off a shelf, one at a time, any more than a husband can marry his lover's mouth and then her bosom and then her neck.

> "...it is impossible for two supreme goods to exist separate from one another. For it is clear that if the two goods are separate, the one cannot be the other, so that neither could be perfect when each is lacking to the other. But that which is not perfect is obviously not supreme... it follows that supreme happiness is identical with supreme divinity."
>
> - Lady Philosophy, 3.10 (p. 71)

When philosophers and theologians speak of God's "simplicity", they do not mean God is "not fancy" or that God is "easy-going." The doctrine of divine simplicity teaches that God has no parts. A man has parts. A man has arms, legs, nose, ears, head, hair, fingernails, and so forth. Some of these parts can be painlessly removed from a man, while the removal of other parts will cause pain, and the removal of others still will cause death. The body itself is part of a man, as is the soul. While the soul is part of a man, the soul itself has no parts. As the soul has no parts, it cannot fall apart, which means the soul cannot die.

Death is always a matter of separation. Bodily death is the separation of the body from the soul. Spiritual death is the separation of the soul from God, as St. Augustine argues in the *City of God*. When a man dies, his body returns to the earth, where space intrudes between the various parts of his body, dividing the parts and making them smaller and smaller until he becomes dust. The soul is the coherence and unity of the body. When the soul departs the body, the body slowly loses its unity. Inasmuch as a thing can fall apart or break, it has a soul. The soul is the image which a thing bears, and every material thing is the incarnation of its own idea. While the soul of man is unique, man is hardly the only created thing which possesses a soul.

To explain this to my students, I often employ one of the pieces of Lego Architecture I keep in my classroom. I hold up a small Lego model of the Sears Tower and ask, "What is this?"

> *Students: A model of the Sears Tower.*
> *Gibbs: How do you know?*
> *Students: It looks like the Sears Tower.*
> *Gibbs: What is it made of?*
> *Students: Blocks.*
> *Gibbs: Yes, the Sears Tower is the soul of the model, and the blocks*
> *are the body. So long as the blocks hold together, they bear the image*
> *of the Sears Tower. But when the blocks come apart, the image of the*
> *Tower becomes obscure.(At this point, I drop the model on a desk and*
> *it fractures into several large pieces)*
> *Gibbs: Is it still the Sears Tower?*
> *Students: …Yes?*
> *Gibbs: But not exactly. The image of the tower has begun to fade as*
> *the Tower is separated into its parts. When I break one part of the*
> *Tower off, empty space intrudes between the parts. The idea which*
> *was impressed on the blocks departs. The blocks are losing their form.*
> *This is what the Lady means when she claims that "everything that*
> *is remains and subsists just so long as it is one, but perishes and dis-*
> *solves immediately it ceases to be one" (p. 74-75).*

When we speak of the departure of the soul from the body we are using figurative language, for the soul has no materiality, and thus the soul is (so to speak) nowhere in particular. A spiritual thing does not have location in quite the same way a physical thing does. Neither does a spiritual thing have a precise position in time, for time is a measurement of motion, and that which is beyond place must necessarily be beyond time, as well. The soul, thus, bears a striking resemblance to God Himself, a fact noted by Anselm of Canturbury in his *Proslogion.* Addressing God Himself, the English theologian writes:

*...no place or time contains you; but you are everywhere and always.
And since this can be said of you alone, you alone are uncircumscribed
and eternal. How is it, then, that other spirits also are said to be uncircumscribed and eternal?*

Anselm concludes his thoughts on the curious similarities between
the soul and God by declaring God "peculiarly uncircumscribed,"
though he offers no explanation of how God transcends other spirits.
It will, perhaps, be enough to say that the transcendence of the human
soul is contingent on divine transcendence; both the human soul and
God exist outside time and space, but the human soul is nonetheless a
creation of God and thus God enjoys priority over creation in His em-
inence. The blessed soul is blessed "by participation" (p. 71) in God, as
Lady Philosophy suggests, though the blessedness of God is underived.

That God's blessedness is underived has profound implications for
human relationships with Him. When I ask students what it means that
God is omnipresent, they typically reply that, "God is everywhere." So,
too, God's omnipotence means "God can do all things" and His omniscience means he "knows all things." These definitions are not bad, for
every week on the way to church, I ask my little daughters, "Where does
God live?" and they say, "Everywhere." I ask them, "What does God
know?" and they say, "Everything." However, these are definitions for
children. When they grow older, they will need meat, not milk.

The difficulty with saying God "knows everything" is that it limits
Him to knowable things. I know some things. I know more things than
an infant, though an infant knows a few things, as well. Older and wiser
persons than myself know more things than I do. If God's omniscience
merely means He "knows everything," His relationship to knowledge is
not qualitatively different from mine. If God "knows everything," His
knowledge is contingent on things and derived from things, much like
my knowledge of things. Similarly, I am somewhere. I am at my desk.
You are somewhere, also. If God is merely "everywhere," He is merely in

more places than I am. If He is everywhere, He can be located in whereness. As a man, I am "here and not there," and if God's omnipresence means He is "everywhere," then God is merely "here and there, too." As a grown man, I occupy more space than an ant, but not as much space as a whale. If God is only "everywhere," He is simply a very large, invisible creature. I have certain powers, as well, and if God's omnipotence is nothing more than His ability to "do all things," His power depends on things to do. God can do things, I can do things, and the number of things God can do is merely greater than the number of things I can do.

In brief, if divine infinitude means nothing more than God's ability to do all things, in all places, at all times, and know all things, He is simply a very large, very powerful, very smart man.

However, the Lady argues that God is goodness itself, time itself, place itself, knowledge itself.

When the rich young ruler approaches Christ in Mark 18, he calls Christ "good teacher" and Christ responds with the claim that "only God is good." Nonetheless, the story of the creation of the cosmos in Genesis declares a great host of things to be good—stars, spheres, the earth, the animals. In the New Testament, Christ speaks of "good ground" and He creates "good wine." In Proverbs, King Lemuel affirms that a good wife is hard to find, but not impossible. So, too, the goodness of a good book is derived from the goodness of God. The goodness of a good apple depends on divine goodness. The goodness of a good writer drafts on God's goodness. God is the form of all good things, and goodness is the means by which all things approach God. All things are embodiments of ideas for which God is the source. Hence, even if a human being could know "all things," he would not have trespassed the divine nature, for God does not merely know all things, God is the very act of knowing. Neither does God merely have the power to do all things, but God is power itself. I might say to a friend, "I will be at the train station at five o'clock today," but when we limit God to being "everywhere," we imply that He will be at the train station at five o'clock, but also at the grocery store and the shoe store and any other place you care to name. But God is being itself, and our being is had in His being, as St. Paul says in the Mars Hill sermon. God is the power by which we *be* at a train station. In the same way we cannot see without eyes, we cannot taste without our tongues, we cannot hear without our ears, we cannot be without God.

The eyes are the instruments of seeing, and God is the instrument of being.

Taking all of these propositions together—that God is being, that God is perfectly unified, that God is simple, that God and God's attributes are indistinguishable, that being and unity and life are the same— Lady Philosophy concludes that "all things desire unity" and "all things seek the good" (p. 77). While it comes as something of a surprise, it is upon this very point which Lady Philosophy turns to show the rule of God. God does not make plans like a man. For a man, a plan is a chronological series of things to do, although a man is distinguishable from his plan. However, God's plans are not distinguishable from Himself. God's plan is God's own self. The unfolding of God's plans are the unfolding of God's very life. A man makes a plan, but things go wrong. It rains, the picnic moves inside, he changes the music because the mood isn't right. However, God's plan and His Person are not distinguishable. God does not make plans. God is His plan. The idea that God has two distinct wills is, for Lady Philosophy, incompatible with a doctrine that God is perfectly unified. What is more, God would not exist in a state of perfect unity were He to possess and create a will which was in conflict with Himself.

**"In the high citadel of its oneness, the mind of God has
set up a plan for the multitude of events. When this plan
is thought of as in the purity of God's understanding, it is
called Providence, and when it is thought of with reference to all things, whose motion and order it controls, it is
called by the name the ancients give it, Fate."**
- Lady Philosophy, 4.6 (p. 104)

A man may live according to Fate or Providence. Lady Philosophy
lays out two ways in which the plans of God may be considered.
When we consider the plans of God as a revelation of God's very being,
He does not so much have plans, but a plan, and His plan is Himself—
considered as such, the Lady calls His plan Providence. However, when
the simple plan of God is considered as diffuse in creation, the Lady
calls it Fate. Fate is not simple, but complex and chronological. Fate
concerns the change which occurs naturally in finite, created things, but
Providence is changeless because God is changeless.

No finite, created man has an intellect spacious enough to consider
Providence. Providence is beyond reason, beyond comprehension, and
man only knows of Providence because it is a logical necessity of Fate.
Aristotle taught that all things are moved by some prior force, and yet,
at the very end of the chain of causality, there must be some unmoved
thing which causes all other things to move. Providence is just such an
"unmoved mover," and Fate is the sum total of all created movement.
Providence is not subject to time and space, though, and so no man can
see it. Fate, on the other hand, can be seen in time. I was fated to write
these words, you were fated to read them, though you could not read
them until I wrote them, which is a rather mundane illustration of how
Fate is chronological.

Surprisingly enough, Lady Philosophy spins these metaphysical
teachings out into moral lessons. She claims, "…certain things which

come under Providence are above the chain of Fate. These are things which rise above the order of change ruled over by Fate in virtue of the stability of their position close to the supreme Godhead" (p. 105). The Lady likens reality to a series of concentric circles, each of which turns, and yet God is the still and motionless center of all the circles. The further away from the Divine center, the greater the turbulence and chaos.

"Anything that joins itself to the middle circle is brought close to simplicity, and no longer spreads out widely. In the same way whatever moves any distance from the primary intelligence becomes enmeshed in ever stronger chains of Fate, and everything is the freer from Fate the closer it seeks the centre of things" (p. 105). The man who draws close to God is freed into Providence, but the man who runs from God is enslaved by Fate.

And yet, how exactly can a man be freed from Fate? Is Fate not, by definition, that from which no one is free?

To answer these questions, we must go back to the beginning of all things.

I would like to begin with the rather standard, rather pedestrian claim that God was under no compulsion to create the cosmos. He did not have to create the cosmos. Rather, God created the cosmos freely and the cosmos bears the imprint of the freedom through which it was created.

God did not create man out of necessity, and so man's very nature is gratuitous, surplus, surfeit. Man's gratuitous nature is his freedom. Had the creation of man been compulsory, man's obedience to God would be likewise compulsory, and yet God presents Himself as a liberator. Biblical descriptions of sin as "bondage" and "slavery" are not primarily judicial; the bondage of sin must be acknowledged as both a physical, psychic, and metaphysical condition. Sin is an incarceration of being. Sin is ontological exile.

Much of the dialogue among Western Christians about sin circles too quickly back to man's "sin nature," which is used to explain every kind of sin from a child's petty theft of candy to the callous methods of the Third Reich. I cannot count the number of times I have caught a student telling lies or spreading malicious gossip, asked them why they would do such a thing and caught the hasty reply, "I have a sin nature. I'm just a sinner," as though sin were the most reasonable thing in the world. Sin nature is the cause, and sinful action the effect. Simple as that.

However, if this discussion of fate is going back to the beginning, we must go back to the original sin. Adam did not sin because he had a sin nature, and neither did Eve. Secularists of our day often address themselves to tragedies with questions of prevention. In the aftermath of a mass shooting, pundits ask, "Did the shooter play violent video games? Did he listen to KMFDM? Was he on antidepressants?" These questions assume that if we can create an ideal place to live, ideal people will emerge from it. Moses teaches otherwise. The sinless Adam, whilst living in a paradise with a spouse who was quite literally made for him, caved to temptation. St. Augustine claimed that inquiring into why Adam sinned is pointless. Sin is not a power, but an absence of power. Sin is not a thing, but a nothing. As such, sin is not a cause of anything, but an anti-cause. Searching for the source of that-which-is-anti-source is a fruitless task. When my daughters sin, there is only one acceptable answer to the question, "Why did you do this?" It is not an answer I taught them, but an intuitive answer a child can always discern in simplicity of heart: *I don't know.*

This is the same reason I sin. I do not know why I do the wicked things I do. No sin has ever worked out well for me, and yet I continue to sin. I do not know why I continue to do things which invariably lead to remorse, self-loathing, the heartbreak of my family, and the embarrassment of my friends. What in the world would prompt a man to hurt himself over and over again? I don't know. Perhaps madness.

I say this not to exonerate myself, for I am perfectly willing to agree with the terms of my own wickedness. My heart is evil. However, claiming "My heart is evil" does not quite get to the heart of the matter. Every man sins for the same reason Adam sinned—but there is no reason Adam sinned. Sin is not reasonable. Sin is opposed to reason. In Book XII of the *City of God*, Augustine claims that Adam made an evil choice, but evil choices proceed from evil wills, and yet Adam's will was good. What was the efficient cause of Adam's evil will, then? The question cannot be answered. "The truth is that one should not try to find an efficient cause for a wrong choice," Augustine writes. "It is not a matter of efficiency, but of deficiency; the evil will itself is not effective but defective."* Put another way, sin does not come from somewhere, but nowhere.

Sin is sin precisely because it comes from nowhere. In other words, sin is arbitrary, and as Dante teaches in the *Paradiso*, man is naturally incapable of arbitrary decisions. It follows, then, that any arbitrary choice is unnatural.

The arbitrariness of sin is a tawdry imitation of the surprising nature of righteousness. Virtue is Surprising, vice is Arbitrary. Seen from a distance, the Surprising and the Arbitrary might be confused for one another. At first blush, both seem to come from an indeterminate place. However, the Surprising derives from the uncircumscribable nature of God, while the Arbitrary derives from nothingness. You see, Nothingness does a good impression of Everything.

Nothingness is an ersatz Everything.

Surprise is the present, unrepeated, and unrepeatable revelation of God. Every kind of Surprise (even common surprises, like a surprise party) references the nature of God, for Surprise is both an event and the fitting emotional response to the infinitude of God. Eternal life is eternal because God is infinite; God dwells in unapproachable light, and yet eternal life is simply the approach unto the unapproachable. Because God cannot be circumscribed, and because He is unapproachable, the finite experience of the infinite is Surprising. Personhood is the right, free action of autonomy. Man's ultimate autonomy is betokened in

---

* *Augustine,* City of God. *Translated by Henry Bettenson. Penguin Classics, 2003. p. 479.*

the unrepeatable quality of each human person. No man is like another precisely because man is free, and man's freedom bears witness to the unapproachable, uncircumscribable nature of God. Personhood is both a gift and an irrevocable covenant God makes with a man to hold that man exclusively accountable for his own will. A man's own personhood is God's vow to hold that man uniquely responsible for himself, in his freedom. Personhood is a covenant God makes with man to judge him. A man may depend on the judgement of God.

Sin is a reversal of personhood, though, for every sin offers a fore-taste of the separation of body and soul which occurs in death. In the beginning, God called order out of chaos by impressing Himself as the Divine Idea on idealess substance. God was not obliged to impress His image on anything, though, and so creation hovers as Surprise over the chaotic sea of Inevitability. Sin is always a kind of materialism, then, because sin is a rejection of the Divine Idea and the attempt to return to a state of pure matter. Materialism and Inevitability are different expressions of the same sinful state. The Inevitable is what *must* happen, what will *surely* happen. The Inevitable is a robbery of autonomy, a robbery of personhood, thus man must sin. However, a man is free to be righteous. Every act of righteousness is Surprising.

Those who find the story of Adam's fall a remarkably predictable affair are quite correct. The man is there, but the forbidden tree is there, as well—how could the story not go the way it does? Does the whole tale of the Fall not funnel the characters inevitably towards the Fall? Sin had to happen. And yet, God does not decree what is Inevitable. God did not create the world out of Necessity. Rather, God created the world freely. He was not compelled to create, thus creation is Surprising, not Inevitable. Man's pursuit of God is no less free than God's pursuit of man. The righteous life is shocking, but the life of sin is compulsory, mandatory. God did not have to create the world, but did so regardless. In doing what He did not have to do, God established Reality as that which is ontologically opposed to Necessity.

If righteousness were predictable, eternal life would not be eternal. What ultimately separates one moment from another or one man from another is the unpredictability of righteousness. Sin renders one man like another; the ultimate goal of Newspeak is a single moaned syllable, a crass imitation of the perfectly simple Word Whose literal meaning is the total value of all reality.

Inevitability is a collapse of free reality into Arbitrary materialism.

It is Inevitable that a man will sin; man *must* sin. There is simply no other antecedent claim strong enough to set up the interrupting Surprise of righteousness. Man must sin, and yet Job was righteous in his trial. It is absolutely *Necessary* that a man sin, and yet Christ did not sin and He was man. Man *must* sin, and yet man is genuinely *free* to be good. Righteousness is opposed to what *must* happen. Creation was not Necessary, and creation was good; sin is both Necessary and Arbitrary. Anything which *must* happen is quite dull.

Nothing I have here written about Inevitability is beyond the bounds of mere psychological realism. Nowhere is sin more easily understood as Inevitability than when we consider a man's besetting sin, a sin which he commits every day and swears off nearly as often. For the drunkard, the Devil never presents liquor as an unfortunate choice the man is free to make, but as a certainty to which the man will obviously surrender. There is no option to drink, but assurance drinking will come to pass. When I ask my students about falling to their besetting sins, they often report—at the ripe old age of sixteen—that their choice in the matter seems to have ended long ago. The fact that we wake from the trance of sin and dismally ask ourselves, "How could I do it again?" speaks to the powerlessness which sin breeds in man. A man asks himself how he could fall to the same rotten temptation once again, because in moments of coherence, he frankly admits he has no desire to commit his besetting sin ever again. Sin is Inevitable because it has nothing to do with our personhood; personhood is renounced in the act of sin. While a man is entirely responsible for his sin, he is also within his rights to say,

"I was not myself when I did it." Such a claim should not be used as an excuse from legal accountability for crimes (every sin must be repented of), and yet, were a happily married man to have an affair and later say, "I cannot believe I did that. In my memory, it seems like someone else did it," he would merely be describing the deleterious effects of sin on the psyche and on consciousness.

On the other hand, what man has not astonished himself by doing the right thing? The man whose soul is caught in a downward spiral does not think to himself, "Anything could happen," for sin dramatically narrows the range of possibilities. Still sheltered from the world, adolescents are surprised by grievous stories of wickedness. However, once a man reaches maturity, evil seems far more tedious. Once I truly understood that some women slaughter their own children, every kind of evil seemed a mere footnote.

When a human being has reduced himself and other human beings to mere material, no degradation is terribly far-fetched. However, righteousness graduates the human spirit into entirely new and unexplored realms of possibility. Holy men forgive the unforgivable. Holy women renounce what is absolutely Necessary and live according to higher laws of being. I have read many stories of St. Nicholas of Myra, including accounts of his raising those long-dead, calming storms, multiplying food supplies, although when I tell my students of St. Nicholas's life, I begin by telling them of his secret gift of money to a poor man who was considering selling his daughters into prostitution. In a world of finite resources, where even Christians are desperately clawing their way to the top, the most pedestrian act of charity is nothing short of a wonder. "Get up, take up your bed, and walk," says Christ to the paralytic, and so miraculous healing and common obedience are one and the same. The dazed feeling which attends besetting sin is a sad forgery of the other-worldly reverie which comes from opening your wallet and handing over all the cash you have on hand to someone with a far-fetched story of need. Such a thing does not feel entirely real. The man handing over the money looks on his own action as though from a third person perspective and says, "What am I doing? I am a rotten person. This does not seem like the kind of thing a rotten person would do." He has escaped Inevitability. He is truly free. In such a state, nothing is impossible for him.

CHAPTER EIGHT

Why Do Anything?

> **Again I saw that under the sun the race is not to the swift, nor the battle to the strong, nor bread to the wise, nor riches to the intelligent, nor favor to those with knowledge, but time and chance happen to them all.**
>
> \- Ecclesiastes 9:11

The average man does not live his life beneath the shadow of death looming darkly overhead, as was the case for Boethius while authoring *The Consolation*, and so what of all the races, battles, bread, and riches the rest of us have to strive for? Boethius will soon be dead, and so he no longer needs to concern himself with being swift and strong. Those who finish reading *The Consolation*, however, must return to their workaday lives, and go back to "the moderate Aristotelian city / Of darning and the Eight-Fifteen, where Euclid's geometry / And Newton's mechanics would account for our experience, / And the kitchen table exists because I scrub it,'" as W.H. Auden put it in "For the Time Being."

If we are not passing all our days in constant prayer, but living predictably mundane lives which are filled with dates, marriages, career changes, Christmas parties, and attempts to write poetry and lose weight and cook like the French, are we doomed to meaninglessness every time Fortune turns her wheel? If the race is not to the swift, what is the point

---

*Auden, W.H. Collected Poems. *Vintage International, 1991. p. 399.*

in becoming swift? If the battle is not to the strong, why train soldiers? Do we live according to chance? Does a righteous man train for the Olympics with his fingers crossed? What is the point in a man spending seven years building a house with his own hands if the house might burn down the night before he moves in? If an Olympic athlete sprains his ankle moments before a gold medal race, has Fortune determined all his preparation and training was for nothing? Is Fortune truly able to reduce a man's life to rubble and ashes? Given the unknowability of the future and the fickleness of fortune, how can a man undertake any great labor without also risking a meaningless life, should his luck turn? Is it possible to live life in such a way that no matter what happens, a man need never say, "It was all for nothing"?

> **"But is there room... for any freedom of the will? Or does the chain**
> **of Fate bind even the impulses of the human mind?"**
> **- Boethius, 5.2 (p. 118)**

> **"...the two seem clean contrary and opposite, God's universal fore-**
> **knowledge and freedom of the will. If God foresees all things and**
> **cannot be mistaken in any way, what Providence has foreseen as a**
> **future event must happen. So that if from eternity Providence fore-**
> **knows not only men's actions but also their thoughts and desires,**
> **there will be no freedom of will."**
> **- Boethius, 5.3 (p. 119-120)**

I n the final book of *The Consolation*, Boethius returns to Epicurus's objection against the doctrine of God's goodness, a philosophical issue inextricably bound up in human freedom. Epicurus's objection to the doctrine of divine goodness is: If God wants to stop evil, but cannot, why do we call Him omnipotent? If God can stop evil, but does not want to, why do we call Him omnibenevolent? If God can stop evil and wants to stop evil, why does evil continue? If God can neither stop evil nor wants to stop evil, why do we call him God? Boethius first references

Epicurus much earlier in the book, in a chapter wherein he is describing the evil done to him by the Roman government, although the reference has little force behind it and is merely made in passing. The Lady is not interested in trying to counter Epicurus without a substantial foundation being laid first, though she is ready to deal in the metaphysics of evil and freedom as her dialog with Boethius draws to a close.

Boethius is concerned that Fate overrides human freedom, that human actions are determined apart from human willing, and thus rewards for the wicked and the righteous are arbitrary. The wicked cannot help being wicked, the righteous cannot help being righteous, and the punishments and rewards of God are no less arbitrary than lottery numbers.

I have no wish to overplay my hand. God's relationship with evil is a deeply vexing matter which Christians have been debating for nearly two thousand years. In the third century, Origen put forth theories of ultimate universal reconciliation between God and all beings, including the Devil, for which he was later condemned as a heretic. In the several centuries which followed Origen, various Church fathers put forth theories of total human reconciliation with God, and while they were not rejected as heretics, neither did they find wide support. Theologians can debate the metaphysics of evil amongst themselves, although the most acrimonious arguments about evil do not take place in universities or seminaries, but in the lonely and troubled hearts of tormented individuals who lay awake at night, wondering why God will not hear their prayers for healing and peace. Far more venerable intellects than my own have committed years of study, contemplation, and prayer to the matter of God's relationship with evil, and yet no perfectly satisfying theological formula has been produced which lays to rest all human doubt. I do not intend, in these pages, to settle the matter of God's relationship with evil once and for all.

However, when I first taught *The Consolation* and finally arrived at the fifth book, which is all about evil and freedom, I could not say that anything of what Lady Philosophy claimed about evil had ever been presented to me. Throughout my teenage years I attended a reformed church; however, I had plenty of Arminian friends at school, as well as teachers who were happy to facilitate disagreements between students on the matter of human freedom and divine goodness. I grew up in a Bible-reading and Bible-believing household, and by the age of twenty-six I had been a member of a dozen different denominations and at no point along the way was the horizon between divine goodness and human freedom ever really sussed out for me. Some might argue that the average Christian does not need to be educated in the finer points of metaphysics. While that claim might have held water in the Medieval era, wherein the average Christian had never met a skeptic, in our own era, a plumber with an ichthys decal on the back of his van is probably going to get asked, at some point or another, why his God let the pipes burst in January.

The Lady is interested in reconciling "God's universal foreknowledge and freedom of the will" (p. 119), but before her explanation will make sense, we must be able to distinguish between apophatic and cataphatic theology, which are two entirely separate ways of thinking and talking of God. Cataphatic language describes God as He appears to us, while apophatic language describes God as He appears to Himself. Cataphatic theology describes God actively, dynamically, as though He were a man capable of emotion, change, fluctuation. When Scripture describes God speaking, moving, mourning, becoming angry, setting His anger aside, and so forth, God is presented as a being which is subject to time. We experience God in time, and thus we sometimes know His anger, at other times His joy, His sadness, or His withdrawing.

On the other hand, apophatic theology describes God as He knows Himself. God transcends time, space, change, and even human attempts to describe Him precisely. Human speech narrows, confines, limits, and demarcates, which are all entirely appropriate actions when directed toward finite things, but any attempt to narrow and confine the infinite is absurd. We can say truly, "God is love," however, no human intellect is capable of wholly comprehending love, and so we must also say, "God transcends love." We can say truly, "God hears our prayers," but we must also say, "God is beyond hearing." These latter statements don't mean God does not love or that He does not hear, but that no human comprehension of love or hearing ascends to the divine height. Apophatic theology might be understood as a kind of speaking silence.

Scripture describes God in both cataphatic and apophatic terms. In Acts 7:48, St. Stephen affirms the prophetic teaching that God "does not dwell in houses made by hands." However, throughout the Old Testament, the "dwelling place" of God is variously affirmed to be the tabernacle or the temple. In Exodus 25:22, God promises to meet the high priest in the tabernacle, in the Holy of Holies, "between the two cherubim that are on the ark of the testimony." So which is it? Does God dwell in houses made by hands or not? A rudimentary knowledge of the difference between apophatic and cataphatic theology rather handily sorts out the apparent discrepancy.

In the past, I have asked students to name all the contradictions in Scripture which they have ever noticed. Many students quickly marry an apophatic claim about the unchanging nature of God with a cataphatic claim about God changing His mind, like the time God "repents of making man" in Genesis, or when His prophet Jonah prophesies the fall of Nineveh and God relents. However, while the claim Christ "increased in wisdom and in stature" (Luke 2:52) and the claim Christ is "the same yesterday and today and forever" (Heb. 13:8) are *literally* at odds with one another, these are two entirely separate species of claims. To use apophatic premises and arrive at cataphatic conclusions creates the illusion of a monstrous God: *God does not change, so there's no point in repenting of your sins. He has either forgiven you already or He never will.* Neither can the doctrine of God's omnipotence be used to justify the idea that "God has caused this or that to happen," for divine omnipotence is a claim that God is beyond doing. Inasmuch as we speak of God "causing this or that to happen," we may speak of creation functioning entirely on its own. God may have done this or that, but the proof is not that He "does everything." Inasmuch as God does some things, He does not do other things. Granted, there are many points of connection between cataphatic and apophatic theology; however, the two must remain distinct from one another in the same way that the human nature of Christ and the divine nature of Christ must remain distinct. The Council of Chalcedon is clear that, theologically speaking, we may not scramble Christ's two natures like the yolk and the white of an egg.

While cataphatic theology is highly anthropomorphic, in truth, apophatic theology is not absent of anthropomorphic claims and analogies to created things. "God sits outside time, unaffected by change" aims for apophatic truth, and yet, the claim nonetheless positions God like an object, even if He has been positioned "outside time." The difference between cataphatic and apophatic language is not metaphorical versus non-metaphorical, but obviously anthropomorphic versus subtly anthropomorphic.

Needless to say, Lady Philosophy believes apophatic knowledge of God transcends cataphatic knowledge. While *The Consolation* is not wholly bereft of cataphatic claims of God, the Lady's Stoic tendencies incline her sympathies toward higher forms of knowledge, and no one would dispute apophatic theology is the way of philosophers and theologians, not the way of the uninitiated. The fact that Scripture employs both manners of describing God by no means suggests they are equal, for some passages of Scripture are easy to understand and some passages quite difficult. As a high school teacher, however, I have found the typical sophomore needs a healthy dose of both. American Christians are apt to say, "It's all about Jesus," rarely reference the Trinity, and often talk of Christ as a friend and a brother Whom we can speak to casually, boldly, and haphazardly. Americans are far less inclined to acknowledge the God who "dwells in unapproachable light" (1 Tim. 6:16) and is He Whom "no one has ever seen" (John 1:18). My interest here is not to remind pacifists and sentimental Christians that God is also a God of wrath, for even those who relish the thought of a God of wrath commonly neglect the many scriptural passages which describe God's incomprehensible transcendence. On the other hand, it is easy to confuse divine impassibility with divine disinterest, and a weak mind might be tempted to see apophatic theology as a declaration that God has nothing to do with creation. In the first several years I taught philosophy and metaphysics, doctrines of divine transcendence swallowed up doctrines of divine love, and I viewed the world as a fundamentally lonely place. A harmonization of cataphatic and apophatic knowledge must take place. This harmonization takes place in the Eucharist, but more shall be said on this later.

Boethius is concerned that God's foreknowledge of future events robs man of his freedom. If God knows a man will sin tomorrow, does that man really have any choice in the matter? The Lady replies that God does not know as a man knows. Man knows chronologically, moment by moment. All things occur in the present. When events of the past occurred, they occurred within their own present, and whenever events of the future ultimately occur, they will also occur within their own present. However, all things occur within the present for God. God sees all things in a continuous, simultaneous present. God sees the creation of the Earth, the dispersion at Babel, the day of Pentecost, the battle of Waterloo, the birth of my wife, the fall of America, and the final Judgement in a changeless tableau as I sit typing these words on a certain January 4th. However, January 4th is by no means "the real day" within the purview of God. For this reason, we must not misunderstand the term foreknowledge. So far as He appears to human beings, God knows what will happen before it happens. However, so far as God regards Himself, there is no before and after, for God is outside time. God does not foreknow anything, for such language makes God subject to time. Rather, God simply knows. God knows reality as it happens, and because all things happen at once, they happen rather slowly. God views creation, the Lady teaches, as a man views a chariot wheel in a race. The

chariot wheel spins and, as it spins, the man knows it; if the wheel stops
spinning, the man knows it has stopped. The man's knowledge of the
chariot wheel spinning does not cause the wheel to spin. So, too, if man
is not God, then God is a "spectator from on high of all things" (p. 137).

In the beginning of *The Consolation*, the Lady tells Boethius that no
man can be exiled from God unless he chooses to be. For the average
teenager, the idea that "God makes His home in the heart of all those
who love Him" sounds like the kind of theological gibberish adults are
obligated to say in order to maintain a semblance of piety, but which has
no genuine value to honest people who truly suffer from dashed dreams
and psychological trauma. The good teacher must save *The Consolation*
from becoming a set of meaningless codes and arbitrary shibboleths at
this point or else his students' eyes will glaze over in disappointment
that they are, once again, being asked to pretend that theology is helpful
and answers important questions.

Before students will understand the idea that God lives in their
hearts, they must know where and what their hearts are. The heart, as I
am employing the term, is not a place from whence evil desires arise. For
the teenager, those desires come from the ungoverned stomach. Teenage
boys do not lust with their hearts, but with their guts. All men return to
their hearts for refuge. I am not speaking of the heart as the emotional
center of a man, but as the ontological and existential center of a man.
When a young man's evil is discovered, and when his parents revoke all
his privileges, he lays down on his bed, perhaps at night, and enters his
own heart.

In his heart, he looks from a great distance out at the world and says,
"You may take away my time, my things, my rights, and my freedoms…
You may force me to do one thing, and forbid me to do another thing…
But you cannot take away my personhood. Though I lose everything,
I am still myself. You may revoke every power I have, but you cannot
take away my thoughts, my freedom to want, and my power to believe
what is right." In many years of teaching *The Consolation*, I have rarely

encountered students who have never been to this place within their hearts. Nearly all of them have discovered their autonomy, their person-hood, the paradoxical place in which the omnipresent God gives sab-bath rest to a rational soul. As Remi Brague writes in "Sin No More":

> *The Sabbath has another, deeper dimension, that we could call a metaphysical one. When the Bible describes God as withdrawing from His work in order to enjoy rest, God is described as free. But the world is, so to speak, free from God's action, too, and is allowed to rest. God does not interfere any more with what He has created. On the contrary, He somehow sets His creatures on a free footing. His providence gives them whatever is required for them to be able to "shift for themselves" in the pursuit of what is good for them.**

The heart is the place where the rest which Brague describes is known and enjoyed. Because God gives sabbath to the human heart, He can truly be a guest there.

The heart is the frontier of God's otherness, and the omnipotent God does not turn up his nose at the role of guest. It is precisely because He is omnipotent that he can play the role of guest and reveal the true essence of a guest. However, when I say that God "plays the role of guest," I am not implying He is less a guest than something else. God is not technically "Lord" and metaphorically "guest." It is only by way of metaphor that God is called "Lord," only by metaphor that He is lamb, rock, or shepherd. It is in this hidden palace of personhood, inaccessible to everyone and everything else, that God is our guest. We more often retreat into our hearts when our fortunes crumble. A man rarely has reason to enter his own heart when the chips are up. Good fortune does not lock the door of personhood from a man's subconscious, though most teenagers are honest enough to admit they only seek freedom

---

* *Brague, Remi. "Sin No More." The American Spectator. Originally published May 1, 2008. Accessed January 5th, 2018: https://spectator.org/42037_sin-no-more/*

within their hearts when their bodies have been confined, restricted, insulted, or wounded. When Fortune begins to take away the world, we hide in that place where Fortune cannot reach.

Given the profound freedom which God has granted us, *The Consolation* returns the Epicurean objection against divine omnibenevolence back upon the one making the objection. Instead of inquiring why God does not stop evil, a man must ask himself, "Are *you* willing and able to stop committing acts of evil?"

In reframing the question as such, I am not suggesting that a man can save himself from Hell. Rather, I am claiming God has empowered the drunk to quit drinking, the adulterer to quit cheating, the liar to quit lying. God has empowered the monster to quit terrorizing his family.

Most discussions of "the problem of evil" depict evil as an impersonal and autonomous force, which evil is most certainly *not*. I am evil, though not by necessity. I do not have to be evil, I am trying not to be evil, though I am not really trying very hard and that is why there is still evil in the world. We may not think of evil as some kind of weather pattern in which man is objectively mired. Evil is not a thing which lifts like a fog. Instead of asking whether God is willing and able to stop evil, we must ask, "Is God willing and able to stop me?" Yes, God is willing and able to knock, to enter, and to dine with you as your guest.

> "Hope is not placed in God in vain and prayers are not
> made in vain, for if they are the right kind they cannot
> but be efficacious. Avoid vice, therefore, and cultivate
> virtue; lift up your mind to the right kind of hope, and
> put forth humble prayers on high. A great necessity is
> laid upon you, and if you will be honest with yourself, a
> great necessity to be good, since you live in the sight of a
> judge who sees all things."
> -Lady Philosophy, 5.6 (p. 137)

Neither the reader of *The Consolation* nor the reader of this slim volume could be blamed for arriving at the final pages and demanding, "What exactly are you suggesting I do with my life?" Everything from hard physical labor to heady sensual pleasure is apt to distract us from the glory and knowledge of God. Hard work, sex and fashion, fine wine, promotions and raises, exercise, wives and children, even a career in politics or the priesthood... Lady Philosophy seems to dismiss anything earthly as ephemeral and unworthy of a creature in possession of an immortal soul. Even the old man who chides his fat, lazy grandson about getting up, getting fit, getting a job and a girlfriend is subject to Lady Philosophy's critiques, for she does not seem to think any more highly of worldly ambition than sloth. Unless a man is going to sit in a dark closet and pray to God until he starves to death, what point is there in doing anything?

At this point, let us stop referring to Lady Philosophy and refer instead to her creator, Boethius.

Boethius shares a good bit in common with Solomon, who began his treatise on the world with a rather bleak assessment of human activity. "What does man gain by all the toil at which he toils under the sun?" he asks in the first chapter of Ecclesiastes. "A generation goes, and a generation comes, but the earth remains forever." Man was created to take dominion over the Earth, but man became a sinner, and now the

Earth takes dominion over man. Cronos ultimately takes back all the buildings, statues, canals, bridges, and monuments he has allowed man to build. Time brings fruit to ripeness, then time brings it to rot. Man is born in time, but finally dies of exposure to time. Trying to gain an advantage over the world, Solomon glibly sighs, is ridiculous.

The Earth always wins. Time always wins. Gravity always wins.

As is the case with Ecclesiastes, however, very little of *The Consolation of Philosophy* is about what we ought to do with our lives, but rather how we ought to do it. Most of my students know that their lives will fall into a rather predictable pattern. They will graduate, go to college, marry, enter a career, have children, live hand-to-mouth for a little while, establish themselves in a field, enjoy a little success, bid their children good luck in the world, retire, attend the funerals of friends, and then their own golden bowls will break and they will go to be judged by God. Between these tentpole events, a few will divorce, a few will become widows, a few will nearly die, and a few will become wealthy or go broke. By the age of thirty, all of my students will learn they have some physical malady (perhaps trivial, perhaps significant) which will need to be tended to and worried about for the rest of their lives. These are the human things. They do not change much. And if none of my students ever quits the world to live as a monk, I will not be discouraged. Students generally turn out like their teachers, claims Christ.

While most of the major events of my students' lives can be anticipated from a long way out, quite a lot remains unknown. One saved man is content to live a predictable life, while another man is broken by a predictable life. One saved man becomes a drunk, another does not. One saved man hides a second life from his family, another does not. One saved man slaps his wife, another does not. One saved man adores his children, another cannot stand his children and invents every possible excuse to spend time by himself. Cronos devours all, but some saved women look forward to their saved husbands coming home in the evening and others do not. While it might be impossible to gain an advantage over the world, not every saved man is as miserable as the next. While it is tempting to claim the misery of sin can be avoided by seeking virtue ("Sinner, stop sinning," the plea of the frustrated pastor), I would like to conclude by offering two less-travelled intellectual pathways to virtue.

One drink is just right, two is too many, three is too few. No small portion of this book has aimed to justify the second and third claims of this proverb, but little has been said of the first. Why is one drink just right? And if so many lives go off the rails because of two and three drinks, how exactly does the one-drink life lead to happiness, virtue, even piety?

Isak Dinesen's remarkable short story "Babette's Feast" recounts how Babette, a French Catholic woman on the run from the law, is accepted into the home of two Danish sisters. The Danish sisters are the relics of a pious Lutheran figure known only as "the Dean," who is the founder of a strictly ascetic religious sect. Little do the sisters know, Babette is one of the finest chefs in the world, though she is unable to demonstrate the full range of her talents for many years. Meanwhile, the sisters eat exceedingly meagre fare and do not drink whatsoever. On the one hundredth anniversary of the Dean's birth (who has since reposed), Babette asks the sisters if she may cook them "a real French dinner," and the sisters begrudgingly assent. A dozen guests attend the meal, one of whom happens to be a well-travelled cosmopolitan and famous general; the general is the only diner in attendance who truly understands the miracle of the dishes which are laid before them, for Dinesen describes the meal as the platonic form of food itself. At the apex of the meal, the general stands to make a speech and the Dean's followers look up to him with "high, happy expectation," for they "were used to seeing sailors and vagabonds dead drunk with the crass gin of the country, but they did not recognize in a warrior and courtier the intoxication brought about by the noblest wine of the world."

For Dinesen, there is no such thing as alcohol. There is gin, and there is wine, but there is also champagne, cognac, stout beers, and lambic ales. They have little in common. Neither are all wines the same. Some wines disgust and degrade, while others ennoble and enlighten. Gin and wine cannot be reduced to "intoxicating beverages," for they are separate materials, incarnations of separate ideas, and thus have separate effects. Neither can all foods be reduced to their caloric value. Eight hundred calories worth of cheap cheddar has little in common with 800 calories of cave-aged Taleggio. Rather, Dinesen understands that every food is a kind of potion which casts a particular spell over the one who ingests it. The enchantment which Christmas dinner casts over a man is entirely different than the spell which hot oatmeal casts over him on a cold January morning. Every pantry is a wizard's closet, every recipe an incantation. A joke is a laughing spell. A sad story is a crying hex. Sophistry is an ignorance curse. All words are magic.

However, Dinesen's "intoxication" does not merely suggest an aesthetics or a gastronomy, but a metaphysics. The Christian holy is not like the pagan holy. The pagan gods were not infinite, but provincial and circumscribable, thus certain places were holy to Zeus because he was present *in those places*, as opposed to other places, where he was not. Holy things might conduct the presence of Zeus, and yet Zeus was not continually present in his holy things anymore than lightning is continually present in flagpoles. For the pagan, the holy is *here, but not there*. The holy is *this, but not that*. Sacred things are set apart from common things, and a chasm sits between the two which cannot be bridged. But no such chasm exists in Christianity, because the Triune God cannot be circumscribed, for at all times and in all places, He fills all things. Within such a schema, a thing is holy because God chooses to manifest Himself through that thing, not because He has exclusively located Himself in that thing. God has vouchsafed to reveal Himself regularly and habitually in certain holy days, holy places, holy ceremonies, holy men, and holy meals, but God is by no means limited to revealing Himself through these things. He is also given to showing up in dreams, the mouths of donkeys, the casting of lots, and the bones of dead men.

While Christianity and paganism both acknowledge the existence of holy things, Christianity does not exactly acknowledge the existence of anything which is merely common or merely secular. No existing thing is entirely devoid of God. Every real thing is at least a little holy.

For just a moment, though, let us call things of lesser holiness "common." Holy things work on a different sort of economy than common things do. The man who eats a whole chicken for lunch has consumed more food than the man who eats only a wing; however, the man who gets a bigger bite of bread at Communion does not receive more grace than the man who gets a little bite. The child anointed with a drop of chrism is not less holy than the man anointed with a thimble full. Genesis is not holier than Jude simply because it is longer. God is known in the simplicity of experience, not the volume of substance. But once we again remove the concept of commonness, we find that every individual thing is a sacrament of itself. Or, as Gerard Manley Hopkins once wrote:*

> *Each mortal thing does one thing and the same:*
> *Deals out that being indoors each one dwells; Selves*
> *— goes itself; myself it speaks and spells, Crying*
> *Whát I dó is me: for that I came.*

A rose is the sacrament of a rose. A knife is the sacrament of a knife. A hot shower is the sacrament of a hot shower. Cutting up an onion is the sacrament of cutting up an onion.

Barely finishing a marathon is the sacrament of barely finishing a marathon. Books and carrots and diamonds and everything "deals out" its own being. Books book a man. Carrots carrot a man. Diamonds diamond a man. A woman womans her husband. All things proffer their spirits, or deal "out that being" that dwells within.

In the Orthodox ritual celebration of the Lord's Supper, each com-

---

* Hopkins, Gerard Manley. "As Kingfishers Catch Fire." 1877

municant comes to the front of the nave, waits in line, and finally receives tinctured bread and wine from a chalice, offered to the tongue of the suppliant on the tip of a bronze spoon. No seconds are offered, neither can the suppliant eat less than the offering. Having presented himself for communion, the suppliant must eat what is given with simplicity. He needs neither more nor less bread and wine than what sits on the spoon. To live sacramentally—acknowledging the omnipresence of a holy God, from Whom all being is borrowed, in Whom all being is sustained, to Whom all being must return—means accepting with simplicity whatever the spoon of reality offers day by day. God has established "a time" for everything which must be done (Ecc. 3), which means the "time to dance" is sanctified for dancing; dancing is the Eucharist of the time to dance. Gathering stones is the Eucharist of the time to gather stones. The Eucharist is a universal experience, for in the Eucharist, the infinite and unconsumable God is consumed. In the nave, the Eucharist binds all together; departing from the nave, the Eucharist is known variously, diversely in all the moments of our lives.

Day by day, God presents us with a time to work, a time to eat, a time to sleep, a time to read to our children. From day to day, tradition, fate, family, society, and the Church have already determined for us what we should do. If a man is willing to be common and to live a common life filled with times and seasons which God makes common to all, he will submit himself to a mysterious, transcendent reality. The infinite Word entered finite history through a finite body. As a finite creature, through finite means, the common man enters the infinite. The man who is ever looking to make himself unique, to distinguish himself from others, to discern and seize the special things of the world—such a man will always isolate himself further and further until he is bereft of companions, bereft of comforters, heroes, and lovers.

The sacrament of the present, the Eucharist of times and seasons, has the power to lift students from some of the most destructive anxieties and fruitless fears which begin creeping into teenage hearts late in high school. The high school sophomore or junior reading *The Consolation of Philosophy* is on the cusp of leaving for college, where there is more freedom and autonomy to be enjoyed than at any other time in life. In college, a man goes where he wants, dates whom he wants, stays up as late as he wants, rises when he wants. He may begin a two-hundred-mile drive to the beach at two in the morning just to see the sun rise over the waves, and he does not need anyone's permission to do so. But, for the time being, the high school senior must ask his mother and father if he is allowed to stay out until ten studying. Is this not absurd? And so the senior shakes and groans, convinced he needs next year's autonomy today.

A human life contains many seasons, many stages, and no matter what stage you are in, there will always come the temptation to believe that the next stage is the one where the good life begins. Just a little more power, a little more freedom, a little more money, and you could be happy.

Junior high students cannot wait until they are old enough to drive, drivers can't wait to date, daters can't wait to graduate, graduates can't wait to move out of the house. Courting couples can't wait to set a date, engaged couples can't wait to tie the knot, newlyweds can't wait until they're not broke. A man enters his career, then he has kids, then he is broke again. People with little children don't like paying babysitters, but older children are a taxing drama all their own. After children move out, a man has retirement to look forward to, and eventually a man is sufficiently old and there is nothing to look forward to. He reflects on these latter years of his life. Of these years, he says, "I have no pleasure in them" (Ecc. 12:1).

The next stage of life is always the one where a man will achieve the perfect amount of autonomy, freedom, and money. Most men pass their lives having never achieved the kind of political clout Boethius had as a Roman consul, but the struggle for greater power and autonomy is foreign to no man. From the moment a child passes into adolescence and becomes self-aware (aware of himself as a sexual being, a free being, an endless range of possible selves), he looks forward to finally shoring up control over all his interests. Unless a man gives up his hope and confidence of a perfectly pleasant tomorrow, he can pass his entire life discontent, anxious, incapable of enjoying any of the blessed "times" which God offers.

If a man believes that good things are just around the corner, he will find it hard to fully invest himself in the present. The present is a thing to be endured, but the future will be enjoyed. He will see the present as ephemeral and passing, while the future will be fixed and eternal. As such, he passes life in a hurry to arrive at the next thing. If work is a means to an end, if the present is merely a means to the future, the present has no value, and neither does human labor. The sacramental present, however, is not merely a work ethic, but a pious zeal for life.

How hard should we work?

Given the Lady's insistence on the ephemerality of all earthly things, the reader of *The Consolation* might finish the book with a dim view of life on earth. However, the Lady never dismisses any human institution or activity apart from the permission of Solomon, who taught, "All is vanity." It is because of the highly unexpected, often unpredictable, plans of God that working hard now either involves great naiveté or great faith, hope. and love. The book of Ecclesiastes opens with the question, "What does man gain by all the toil at which he toils under the sun?" The more confrontational way of wording the question is, "Why do anything at all?"

The question is honest, not rhetorical. If a man is honest with himself, he can probably admit that on occasions wherein his good deeds are repaid with scorn, or when his time and labor unfairly crumble to ash in his hands, he seriously questions whether anything is worth doing. He considers fourth-century Christians who departed cities in droves and lived in isolation, praying, eating little, sleeping little, and he wonders if he should do the same. A man plants a field, waters it, tends it, but a late drought reduces his field to a pile of wilted, fruitless shrubs before he harvests anything. Another man spends years building a house brick by brick, accrues no debt, but the house burns to the ground the evening before he planned to move in. An unfair admissions board ends dreams of attending the ideal college. An elderly couple save for years so they can travel to Europe for the first time, but a hurricane damages their home and zeroes out their savings account. A young woman dreams of motherhood, but is diagnosed with terminal cancer at nineteen. Everyone has suffered dashed hopes, and not hopes dashed on foolishness or vice, but hopes dashed on bad luck and sudden unpreventable tragedy. Given the fragility of life, why do anything at all? Why try? Is the man who undertakes to build a house, to train his body, or win the heart of a woman not a little too innocent, a little too trusting, for not understanding the arbitrary ways in which the world unsettles us all, from time to time, without warning or concern?

Solomon is upfront about the mutability of hard work. In Ecclesiastes 9, we are told:

> *Again I saw that under the sun the race is not to the swift, nor the battle to the strong, nor bread to the wise, nor riches to the intelligent, nor favor to those with knowledge, but time and chance happen to them all.*

This is not really the way the hard worker wants the world to function, though. The race should be to the swift, the battle to the strong, the scholarship to the studious. Is this not fair? Is it not sufficiently hard to become the swift—but if the race is not even to the swift, what is the point in being swift? If the battle is not to the strong, what is the point in training hard?

What is striking, though, is that right before Solomon declares that bread is not to the wise, nor favor to men of knowledge, he says something that will confound the faithless: *Whatever your hand finds to do, do it with all your might.*

Why?

In C.S. Lewis's *The Screwtape Letters*, the elder demon Screwtape suggests to his young apprentice Wormwood that God wants His people to live in the present, where he has placed them, or in eternity, where he has destined them. Screwtape suggests that Wormwood get his patient (the human being whom the demon is assigned to tempt) to dwell on the future.

Constant rumination on the future leads to Hell, according to the Screwtape.

> *Gratitude looks to the Past and love to the Present; fear, avarice, lust, and ambition look ahead... [God] does not want men to give the Future their hearts, to place their treasure in it. We do. [God's] ideal is a man who, having worked all day for the good of posterity [if that is his vocation], washes his mind of the whole subject, commits the issue to Heaven, and returns at once to the patience or gratitude demanded by the moment that is passing over him. But we want a man hagridden by the Future—haunted by visions of an imminent Heaven or hell upon earth... We want a whole race perpetually in pursuit of the rainbow's end, never...happy now, but always using ...every real gift which is offered them in the Present... as mere fuel wherewith to heap the altar of the Future.*

If Wormwood can convince his patient to labor now for what he believes will come to him, he will have taken his patient to the point where earthly things give value and worth to earthly things—God is entirely locked out of the economy of desire. The prize for which we run, as St. Paul teaches, has been smuggled out of view. If a man comes to believe that his hard work entitles him to a house, or that his decent poetry entitles him to a wife, or that his lucid intellect entitles him to a book deal, none of these things can be acknowledged as the undeserved gifts of

God. They are not Eucharistic, for there is no one to be thanked. Rather, a simple, but fair exchange of goods has taken place. There is no gift, only payment. The man who has earned it need not preface anything he says with, "If the Lord wills," because his work has entitled him to speak on God's behalf. His work has made him god.

A god allows a man to understand the world from a cosmic standpoint, not merely a fleshly, earthly standpoint. Your god is whatever interprets your life. Your god is whatever gives your life meaning. Your god is whatever stands behind the answer you give any time you are asked "Why?" Athenians served Athena and Apollo because they trusted order, prosperity, life. Health came from these gods. At the point Athenians could no longer trust their gods for these goods, their gods died.

The Christian God does not hide Himself from us in our work and in adversity only to reveal Himself when we receive the rewards for our work. In Him we live and move and have our being, thus He is revealed both in our work and in our reward. The love of God is the essential task of every moment of our lives. Loving God and working out our salvation with fear and trembling is hardly a task for which we must await payment. If a man labors out of love for God, he does not have to wait anxiously to see if his work will pay off. His work is paying off as he does it. If the field he has planted is destroyed by drought, or if the house he has built collapses, the man who has labored for the love of God will never look back on his years of labor and sigh over a meaningless life. The love of God is the meaning of his life. The point of planting the field was not planting the field. The point of building the house was not building the house. The point of eating the Eucharist is not to quell hunger. The field is planted so a man might know God in the planting.

However, if a man labors for pay and pay alone, pay is his god. Pay supplies his labor with value, and when that pay ultimately fails him, his god will die. Regardless of the creed he professes, the man who labors for earthly goods is simply biding his time before confessing himself an atheist.

But what does it mean to labor out of love for God? Does it mean praying ceaselessly? Must God dominate our conscious thought as we do a thing in order for that thing to be done "for the Lord"?

The book of Ecclesiastes has contributed a number of pithy phrases to the contemporary Christian lexicon, although the most common and misunderstood is "under the sun." "Under the sun" is not a euphemism for all reality, but for life on earth, life in the saeculum, the world we see with our eyes. Solomon writes, "Then I considered all that my hands had done and the toil I had expended in doing it, and behold, all was vanity and a striving after wind, and there was nothing to be gained under the sun" (Ecc. 2:11) And again, "…what is done under the sun was grievous to me, for all is vanity and a striving after wind" (Ecc. 2:17) And again, "What has a man from all the toil and striving of heart with which he toils beneath the sun?" (Ecc. 2:22) And again, "then I saw all the work of God, that man cannot find out the work that is done under the sun" (Ecc. 8:17). The expression is used twenty-nine times in the book of Ecclesiastes and by the end of the book, the picture Solomon has painted of life under the sun is biting, hopeless, even terrifying.

However, the expression "under the sun" is not comprehensive, for there is world above the sun, as well. The work of angels and seraphim in Glory is not bleak, not pointless. If a man would escape a hopeless, pointless life under the sun, he must be delivered of the domination of the sun. The great difference between a vain life and the life of eternal consequence, to which Christ calls us, is this: *The Christian life must not be lived under the sun. The Christian life is lived above the sun.*

In the Old Testament, sacrifices were offered to God by way of immolation, or burning. The smoke of the sacrifice on the altar was a sweet-smelling aroma offered to God, which ascended to God and was received by Him in Heaven. Burning was not simply a way of destroying a sacrifice, as though the Israelites had to show God they didn't *need* their animals anymore. If this was the case, burying a sacrificial animal would have worked, or casting the sacrificial animal into the ocean. However, the immolated sacrifice was returned to God, handed back to Him.

This immolation looked forward to Christ, Who fulfilled the sacrificial system as our perfect paschal Lamb. The sacrifice of Christ is our life and, for the last two thousand years, we have been called to follow him to the Cross, to live a life of sacrifice, to ascend over the sun and be received into the arms of God, not merely at the end of our lives, but in all that we do, day by day, time after time, season after season. In Romans 12, St. Paul commands that we "present your bodies as a living sacrifice, holy and acceptable to God, which is your spiritual worship."

The concept of a "living sacrifice" certainly struck first-century ears quite strangely. There had never been such a thing spoken of before. Sacrifices were, by their very nature, dead on behalf of the living. And yet our life in the living Christ, our life in the living paschal sacrifice, allows us to be "living sacrifices," as well.

The vaporous, fleeting life is a life without sacrifice, a life not offered as sacrifice. A life destroyed, but not converted to smoke. A life which never ascends into the heavens over the sun from the altar of self-denial and love. The vain life is not offered up to God, but to some earthly good or earthly pleasure in the future. The vain life never ascends higher than the Harvard classroom, the bank, the dance floor, the soccer field, the home or the classroom.

Further, God does not desire sacrifice because He likes to see His image or His good creation destroyed. We serve the God who wants to "make all things new," and we know that the path to making all things new is the path to Golgotha, where we are all commanded to take our crosses every day. When our lives are lived sacrificially, they are not lost. They are not destroyed. Instead, our imperfect lives ascend above the sun where God majestically sanctifies them, remakes them, and makes them whole. All of your life is a gift, which means all your life is fodder for gifts which can be given to others. All of your life is a gift, which means you don't have to deal with the stress and anxiety of holding on tightly to anything other than Jesus Christ.

What I'm suggesting here is not that you should give no thought for your future. You should give great thought to your future, but not because it will help you secure your future. Thinking of the future is merely the work of the present. Thought for the future reveals what justice, wisdom, courage, faith, hope, and love look like today, the day in which God has called you to love Him, serve Him and serve Him in others.

Do you want your children to go to college? Do you want to leave them an inheritance when you die? This is good. These desires reveal to you what obedience looks like today. That obedience is what your "hand has found to do," as Solomon might say. Obey mightily. God alone holds your future, which frees you to zealously, tenaciously throw yourself into loving with your whole heart now. Christians do not hunger on Tuesday for meals served on Wednesday. Christians know that God is present everywhere, at all times, and the present moment is a gift God has given you that you might have something to return to Him. For everything there is a season and a time, so when God gives you time to teach, teach with your whole heart. When God gives you time to sleep, sleep as deeply and luxuriously as you can. When God gives you time to mourn, cry your eyes out. When God gives you a time to laugh, exhaust yourself in laughter. When God gives you a time to share in the lives of others, don't hold anything back for yourself. Pour yourself out, and rise to Glory way over the sun.

ACKNOWLEDGEMENTS

I would like to thank Doug Jones, whose short fiction class set me to writing stories, for stories were my way into teaching. I am also greatly in debt to Peter Leithart, my friend and former pastor, who is the model of a generous intellectual, which I have been struggling to imitate for nearly two decades now. This book would not have been possible without Jon Paul, whose brilliant conversation over the years has refined me, and to whom this book is dedicated. I could not fail to mention Matt Yonke and David Dalbey, for they kept me sharp in the years when everything else was dull. Many thanks also to Keith Nix and Robyn Burlew, whose friendship and support at Veritas has made this book possible. For my parents, both thanks and apologies: thanks for buying me a classical education, apologies for shirking my duties for so long. And finally, all my love and thanks to Paula, the black monolith to my David Bowman.